Basque Topics Series No. 1

The Bombing of Gernika: A Short History

Xabier Irujo

Center for Basque Studies
University of Nevada, Reno

*This book is published with the generous financial
assistance of the Basque Government*

Basque Pocket Books Series, No. 1

Center for Basque Studies

University of Nevada, Reno

Reno, Nevada 89557

http://basque.unr.edu

Book design by Daniel Montero

All photos courtesy of the Documentation Center of the Bombing of

Gernika, Gernika, Bizkaia

Library of Congress Cataloging-in-Publication Data

Names: Irujo Ametzaga, Xabier, author.
Title: The bombing of Gernika : a short history / Xabier Irujo.
Other titles: Bombing of Guernica
Description: Reno : Center for Basque Studies, University of Nevada,
[2018]
    Series: Basque pocket series ; No. 1 | Includes bibliographical refer-
ences
    and index.
Identifiers: LCCN 2018039513 | ISBN 9781935709916 (pbk. : alk.
paper)
Subjects: LCSH: Guernica (Spain)--History--Bombardment, 1937.
    Spain--History--Civil War, 1936-1939--Aerial operations, German.
    Spain--History--Civil War, 1936-1939--Aerial operations, Italian.
Classification: LCC DP269.27.G8 I77 2018 | DDC 946.081/4--dc23
LC record available at https://na01.safelinks.protection.outlook.
com/?url=https%3A%2F%2Flccn.loc.gov%2F2018039513&-
data=01%7C01%7C%7C2f46c4b03639402e283008d62e2ce4ed%7C523b
4bfc0ebd4c03b2b96f6a17fd31d8%7C1&sdata=K6emGAqPnWik-
GCAB6mUP0zrR6btXkAZYo5%2Bs%2FPUf8wA%3D&re-
served=0

Contents

Under the Oak
of the Basques

On October 7, 1936, the first Basque lehendakari or president of the modern era, Jose Antonio Agirre, took his oath of office under the Oak
of Gernika, an eternal symbol of Basque independence, spirit, and resolve.

> *Jainkoaren aurrean apalik,*
> *Eusko Lur gainean zutunik,*
> *asaben gomutaz,*
> *Gernikako Zuhaizpean,*
> *herri ordezkarion aintzinean*
> *nere agindua ondo betetxea zin dagit.*

> Humble in front of God,
> Standing in our Basque lands,
> Remembering our heritage,
> under Gernika's venerable tree,
> as president of my country,
> I swear to serve my term faithfully.

It was a silent and solemn moment in a time of great crisis and unease. Fascist nationalist rebels had risen in revolt against legally constituted Spanish and Basque governments. But for a busy Basque market town and traditional seat of the Basque laws, the solemn oath would have been just an exciting break in an already otherwise busy life between farm, market, trade, friendship, love—the normal activities of a town, the playing and running of children, the conversations, games of pelota and *mus*. War was out there, beyond, a shadow lurking beyond the horizon, but in this beautifully situated town in the hills, daily life continued uninterrupted . . .

Prehistory of Terror Bombing

Cities have been bombed for a long time, even before the invention of airplanes. Henry T. Coxwell, an English aeronaut, launched the first bomb from a hot air balloon in 1848. On August 1849, during the Italian war of independence, the first aerial bombardment was recorded. On that occasion, the Austrian artillery General Franz von Uchatius sent several self-controlled balloons armed with fifteen kilos of explosive ready to deflate automatically over Venice from the ships that besieged the city.

By 1899 there had been so many air attacks on urban centers that the First Hague Convention banned aerial bombardments.

The first aerial bombardment of a ground target from a heavier-than-air aircraft took place in 1911, eight years after the Wright brothers invented the self-propelled aircraft.

On that occasion the second lieutenant Giulio Gavotti of the Italian colonial army decided to put four 2-kilogram grenades full of picric acid (TNP) in a bag and throw them over the oasis of Tagiura in Libya from a Taube monoplane during the War of Tripolitania.

After the Zeppelin terror bombing campaign of World War I, an event marked the history of aerial bombardment in 1919 when Amanullah Khan declared the independence of Afghanistan, which ignited the Third Afghan War. The British expeditionary troops, depleted due to the budgetary adjustments after the Great War, could barely withstand the attacks of the insurgents. After bombing Dakka and Jalalabad, the British command decided to experience a new type of war: to send a single plane, a Handley Page V/1500 called Old Carthusian, to bomb Kabul. The operation was carried out on May 24. The bomber, piloted by two people, launched four 50-kilogram, sixteen-pound bombs on the emir's palace. The attack caused a great psychological impact and, after a series of bombings, the emir's troops capitulated at the beginning of June.

The message was resounding: the British had won a war by using a single plane, in a six-hour operation, without counting any losses. The financial cost of the operation was minimal, the efficiency absolute and the time, record. The European administrations began to invest in bombing planes and experts in aerial warfare developed theories about new concepts such as "mechanical army," "strategic bombing," and "total war." A new way of waging war had been invented: terror bombing.

In the 1930s, all European administrations seriously promoted the development of the military aeronautical technology. The "skin-metal" aircraft, the closed cabins, the retractable landing gears, the bomb-carriers and, fundamentally, the increase in the destructive power of the bombs were some of the achievements resulting from the generous public investment in armament.

As Stanley Baldwin expressed in the British parliament in 1932, in view of the political program of German national-socialism and the expansionism of the Italian and Japanese regimes, "I think that it is well for the man in the street to realize that there is no power on earth which can protect him from being bombed. Whatever people may tell him, the bomber will always get through . . . . The only defence is in offence, which means that you have to kill more women and children more quickly than the enemy if you want to save yourselves."[1]

---

1. Stanley Baldwin, House of Commons, November 10, 1932. John J. Weltman, *World Politics and the Evolution of War* (Baltimore: Johns Hopkins University Press Press, 1995), 101.

3

Brünhild and Sigfried in 1936

In July 1936 Generals Francisco Franco and Emilio Mola were in charge of an army of insurgents who had orchestrated a coup d'état against the democratic government of the Spanish Republic. Franco had at his command more than thirty thousand men in the Spanish colonies of Morocco but most of the officers of the Spanish navy remained loyal to the republican government, therefore, Franco could not transport these men by ship to the Iberian Peninsula and advance toward Madrid. The only means of transporting the troops was to create an airlift from Northern Africa to the Tablada Airfield near Seville, but Franco did not have airplanes and lacked pilots.

Franco and Mola therefore requested military and strategic assistance from their natural allies, António de Oliveira Salazar in Portugal,

Adolf Hitler in Germany, and Benito Mussolini in Italy. And they all agreed to help the rebels.

A week after the coup d'etat, Franco ordered Captain Francisco Arranz to go to Berlin and request a shipment of Junkers Ju 52. When Arranz arrived, Hitler was not there. On July 25 Hitler was in Bayreuth, attending the performance of Wagner's Siegfried directed by Wilhelm Furtwängler in Villa Wahnfried, the birthplace of the German composer. The third act of Siegfried represents the heroine Brünhild enclosed within a magical circle of fire by Wotan, from which only the kiss of a hero can rescue her. There is only one requirement, the said hero could be no coward; only a fearless man could break the circle of magical fire and awaken the heroine. Siegfried arrives at the place and sounds his horn strongly thus destroying the spell that keeps the circle of fire active. Upon crossing the fire, Siegfried kisses Brünhild who awakens from the dream that has held her captive for seventeen years. And they love each other.

Arranz's request came just after Hitler left the opera. Franco was not a Nazi and Hitler was not a National-Catholic, but a strong feeling of anticommunism and contempt for democratic values united both leaders. In record time, and against the opinion of the majority of the officers of the German army's General Staff and the opposition of the foreign ministry Konstantin von Neurath, Hitler agreed to help the coup plotters. Hitler thus became Franco's Siegfried, and Franco Hitler's Brünhild. On July 27, ten days after the military coup, Hitler sent Franco six Heinkel He 51 and twenty Junkers Ju 52.[1] These first Junkers and their forty-two crew members were under the command of Lieutenant Rudolf von Moreau who months later would participate in the bombing of Gernika.

By April 17, 1937, nine days before the bombing of Gernika, the German government had sent Franco a total of 157 aircraft, 46 percent of the Francoist air force in April 1937. Of these 157 planes, 87 had been deployed to the Basque front, that is, 55.4 percent of the total units of the Condor Legion were operating in the Basque Country in April 1937: 35 bombers, 34 fighters, 17 reconnaissance aircraft, and 1 liaison plane.[2]

Coinciding with the creation of the Condor Legion, Hitler appointed the minister of the air Hermann Göring director of the Four Years Plan, the office in charge to prepare Germany for the "next war" between 1936 and 1940. According to the plan, the Luftwaffe would have by the fiscal year 1940–1941 fourteen thousand aircraft organized into a thousand squadrons, each equipped with nine aircraft, three in reserve and two for training. Göring became one of the most determined supporters of Spanish

1.   Xabier Irujo, *Gernika 1937: The Market Day Massacre* (Reno: University of Nevada Press, 2014), 18.

2.   Ibid., 29.

intervention since the war offered him an opportunity to become the second strong man of the Reich. By early 1938 Göring had convinced Hitler that the next war would be won from the air and became Hitler's successor. Göring's salary multiplied by five between 1935 and 1940. Whereas at the beginning of World War II the salary of a Reich minister or that of an admiral or field marshal was between 25,000 and 48,000 RM (with the addition of extra pay and compensation), the salary of Herr Göring rose above all others to around 240,000 RM per year (approximately $1.7 million per year in 2016 dollars), in addition to other more substantive revenues obtained through the theft of works of art and real estate or the dubious investment of public funds.[3]

Apart from geostrategic, ideological, and economic reasoning, Hitler decided to intervene in favor of Franco in order to test his army. Germany had a powerful armed force, but it had never entered combat. The United Kingdom and the French Republic had actively experimented with their air forces in the Middle East between 1919 and 1936 but Germany, which had lost all of its colonies at the end of the World War I, had not had the chance to tests its new machines in combat. As a consequence, while the rest of the European powers experienced new bombing systems in their transoceanic colonies

---

3.   Xabier Irujo, *Gernika: 26 de abril de 1937* (Barcelona: Crítica, 2018), 37-52.

Colonel Wolfram von Richthofen, chief of staff of the Condor Legion.

in Africa and, especially, in the Middle East, the German pilots lacked combat experience. The Spanish war would allow the German command to experiment and put to the test the war material of the Luftwaffe while the crews gained combat experience. Thus, the main mission of the Condor Legion was to experiment new war strategies, fundamentally new bombing systems, and prepare the Luftwaffe for World War II. As the American consul in Bilbao William Chapman expressed in a report to Ambassador Claude Bowers in June 1937, German aviators had the opportunity to prove the usefulness and destructive capacity of their aircraft and in this way Germany and Italy turned Spain into a testing ground.[4]

Göring gave the command of the Condor Legion to General Hugo Sperrle and Sperrle appointed Colonel Wolfram von Richthofen as chief of staff of the Legion. Sperrle and Richthofen were two diametrically different characters. Colonel Wilhelmi, a fellow German officer, described Sperrle as a terrible person: "Sperrle, like a bear, very tall and almost 200 kilos! With his big monocle and stomach ulcer, he spoke neither Spanish nor French, he was always threatening with court-martials."[5] In fact, Hitler himself said of Sperrle that, along with General Reichenau, he was one of his two "most brutal-looking" generals.[6] Hitler even ordered Sperrle to attend the meeting that would take place in Berchtesgaden on February 12, 1938 with the Austrian delegation in order

---

4. Memorandum of the US cónsul in Bilbao William E. Chapman to the US ambassador Claude G. Bowers. Donibane Lohitzune, June 14, 1937. NARA, Bilbao Consulate General Records (1936–1946). Box 4, 1937.

5. Letter of the retired coronel Wilhelmi to Jesús Salas. Barcelona, November 21, 1967. AHEA, A-2125. Richard Brett-Smith also described Sperrle as an "enormous, solid, and ferocious looking" person. Richard Brett-Smith, *Hitler's Generals* (San Rafael, CA: Presidio Press, 1976), 124.

6. Samuel W. Mitcham, *Hitler's Commanders: Officers of the Wehrmacht, the Luftwaffe, the Kriegsmarine, and the Waffen-SS* (Lanham, MD: Rowman & Littlefield, 2012), 113.

General Hugo Sperrle, commander of the
Condor Legion.

to execute the Anschluss. Sperrle was ordered not to open his mouth and to stare through his monocle at the members of the delegation. And, indeed, after the February 12 meeting, Austria was incorporated into the Reich. The massive appearance of Sperrle, his thick neck, ferocious physical qualities, and his usual monocle made of him the perfect caricature of a Prussian general in Hitler's view.

However, Sperrle never was a member of the Nazi party. His chief-of-staff, Richthofen, on the other hand, an aeronautical engineer, was a silent, methodical, and extremely cruel person. From an early age he was an admirer of Hitler and an active member of the Nazi party. He took part as a speaker at various events of the party and was one of the few high-ranking officers of the Luftwaffe who in 1945 continued to support the Führer. His methods did not always conform to the laws of war and committed atrocities such as war experiments and terror bombing campaigns from 1936 to 1945. In the course of the Battle of Stalingrad, the Luftwaffe held an indeterminate number of Soviet prisoners in a hangar. After several days without food, water, or warm clothes, Richthofen was informed of the situation and ordered they to be kept in such circumstances indefinitely.[7] Indeed, Richthofen's main task as chief of staff of the Condor Legion was to experiment new methods of warfare and develop new strategies and techniques of bombing on the battlefield, which was in itself a violation of the laws of war since open cities were often targeted causing large numbers of casualties among civilians.

In order to demonstrate that the air force would be the decisive weapon in the course of the next war, Richthofen had to achieve something that neither the navy nor the ground forces could achieve such as the total destruction of a city in less than three hours. This experiment

---

7.   James S. Corum, *Wolfram von Richthofen: Master of the German Air War* (Lawrence: University Press of Kansas, 2008), 25.

would demonstrate that the next war would be won from the air and that, therefore, the air force was the most powerful weapon of the Reich. General Göring was naturally very interested in putting this theory to the test, for if he convinced Hitler that he was in possession of the most powerful weapon in the Reich, he would have a better chance of being named Hitler's successor.

Gernika, like many other Basque, Catalan, and Spanish towns, thus became the proving ground of Franco's aviation.

With the help of the deposed king Alfonso de Borbón, exiled in Rome, the coup leaders led by Generals José Sanjurjo and Emilio Mola had contacted Mussolini after the elections of February 1936 and the Duce agreed to assist the rebels when the time came. However, when in July he was notified that General Franco had rebelled, he doubted, since Sanjurjo had died just four days after the coup and nobody knew Franco or had negotiated anything with him in the spring of 1936.

The aerial units of the Italian air force that Mussolini sent to Franco acted under the name of Aviazione Legionaria led by General Vincenzo Velardi. The Italian command had 147 aircraft at war on April 17, 1937, nine days before the bombing of Gernika: 32 bombers, 77 fighters, 31 reconnaissance aircraft, and 7 seaplanes. All this accounted for 43 percent of the aircraft available to General Franco in April

1937.[8] Of these 147 airplanes, 73 were destined in the aerodromes of Soria, Vitoria-Gasteiz, and Logroño (49.6 percent of the total) deployed to act in the Basque front.

In April 1937, 89 percent of the planes in General Franco's service were German or Italian piloted by German or Italian crews, and 50 percent of these forces were operating in the Basque Country.[9]

However, all the foreign air units that fought for General Franco operated directly under his orders, so that they could not act independently. In fact, according to the ordinances of the air forces, Franco was the only one who could order aerial bombardments on urban nuclei.[10] The bombing of Gernika, as well as each and every one of the more than a thousand bombing operations that the Francoist command executed in the Basque Country between July 1936 and August 1937, was ordered directly by the Generalissimo.

---

8.   Irujo, *Gernika 1937*, 15.

9.   Ibid., 29.

10.   Orden para la colaboración y apoyo de las fuerzas aéreas con las brigadas de Navarra. 29 de marzo de 1937. AGMA, box 2585, folder 71.

4

The Non-Intervention Committee

The European powers did not want to provoke a general European war and opted for a policy of appeasement by granting political or strategic advantages to Germany and Italy. The German high command and Hitler himself also understood that they were not prepared to face "the new war" until 1940, as established by the Four Year Plan led by Göring from 1936.

Under these circumstances, the French government led by Léon Blum persuaded the British government led by Stanley Baldwin to offer Hitler and Mussolini a non-intervention agreement regarding the Spanish conflict. Under the agreement, no one would send any type of military aid to any of the two parties at war. This fact was favorably received by the German and Italian regimes that signed the agreement without intending to comply with it.

*German pilot next to a Heinkel He 51
ground attack plane.*

In fact, Mussolini did not fully decide to support the coup leaders until August 1936 when he learned that the French and British governments were willing to sign a non-intervention agreement: the settlement guaranteed the victory of the coup leaders since while the Spanish Republic would not receive any help from the European democratic powers, the rebels would be supported militarily and strategically by fascist Italy, Nazi Germany, and the Portuguese regime of Oliveira Salazar.[1] When Italy and Germany joined the non-intervention system on August 17, 1936, both regimes had already decided and initiated the process

---

1.   Paul Preston and Ann L. Mackenzie, eds., *The Republic Besieged: Civil War in Spain 1936-1939* (Edinburgh: Edinburgh University Press, 1996), 41-42.

of sending war material and large-scale troops twenty-two days before, starting on July 25. As noted by British reporter George L. Steer, when Karl G. Schmidt, a twenty-one-year-old radio-telegraphist, was captured after his plane was shot down in January 1937 on the Basque front, the soldiers who took him prisoner discovered that his silk parachute had been produced in a German factory on an interesting date—just twenty-four hours before the adoption of the non-intervention agreement by Hitler![2]

And the British and French administrations were perfectly aware of the troops and armament that the future Axis powers were shipping to Franco. In fact, the British intelligence services intercepted all radio emissions of the Italian command, so that the British Ambassador Sir Henry Chilton received, duly translated into English, each and every one of the cables that the Italian General Staff sent from Salamanca to Rome. And the transcriptions lay today in the shelves of the British National Archives at Kew.

Everything related to the system of non-intervention was false. The non-intervention agreement was not a treaty since there was no written copy of it, it was never signed and its objective was not "non-intervention" but to control the intervention of the German and

2.   George L. Steer, *The Tree of Gernika: A Field Study of Modern War* (London: Hodder and Stoughton Ltd., 1938).

Italian forces in order to avoid an open international conflict. It was an oral pact under which twenty-four European governments pledged not to intervene or sell or send arms to either side at war. The manifest violation of the agreement forced all the administrations involved in it to lie to the press and to their own fellow citizens and institutions and the war, a prologue to the Second World War, came to be emphatically called "Spanish Civil War" when it clearly was an international conflict.

US Ambassador Claude Bowers accused in his August 30 1937 report addressed to Secretary of State Cordel Hull the farce of the non-intervention committee:

> The Non-intervention Pact was proving itself a dishonest farce. The Fascist powers fought just openly, defiantly, with arms; most of the democracies fought just as effectively, if unconsciously, as collaborationists of the Fascist under the mocking cloak of "non-intervention." When men of good minds assumed that Italy, Germany, and even Portugal were observing the pact, the dishonesty of the pretense stood out like a sore thumb. This pact has become a mockery by October 1936. It denied the Spanish government arms and ammunition while turning a blind eye to the

Hitler became one of the first allies of General Franco.

glaring violations by Germany and Italy. Arms and ammunition poured into Portuguese ports, and without inspection at the customs were hurried through to Franco's forces. It was common knowledge. Later, deliveries were made openly through Cádiz, Vigo, Passejas,[3] and Malaga. On September 16, 1935,[4] John Whittaker, Hubert R. Knickerbocker, and Floyd Gibbons,

3.   Pasaia in Basque or Pasajes in Spanish.

4.   1936.

> war correspondents, informed me
> that rebel aviation consisted largely of
> German bombers and Italian pursuit
> planes, and that in Seville they had
> seen German officers in the cafés.[5]

And Bowers added that in the shoddy days when certain British ministers were assuring in the House of the Commons, on their responsibility as ministers of the Crown, that they had "no information" while they were aware of the contrary.[6] The same may be said of Senator Key Pittman of Nevada, chairman of the Committee on Foreign Relations, who once and again claimed at the US Congress that there was no evidence to indicate that the Italian or the German regimes were supporting the rebels.[7]

The German and Italian air units, under the names of Legion Condor and Aviazione Legionaria, covered their airplanes with badges and fake insignia in order to reconcile the interests of the Non-Intervention Committee. In theory, they were "troops of volunteers" who flew with their own planes and bombs to fight for Franco and against international communism. The planes of both armies sported white

---

5.   Claude Bowers, *My Mission to Spain* (Paris: Flammarion, 1956), 325.

6.   Ibid.

7.   Congressional Record. Proceedings and debates of the First Session of the First Session of the 75th Congress of the U.S.A. Volume 81, Part 3, March 18, 1937, to April 16, 1937, USGPO, Washington, 1937, p. 3317.

blades on a black background on the wings and the fuselage and black blades on a white background on the tail instead of the insignia and colors of the military units of both regimes. The German units were identified with the number 88 because "H" is the eighth letter of the alphabet: 88 meant "HH" or "Heil Hitler."

This tragic farce would give rise to the expression coined by the British journalist Claud Cockburn "never believe anything until it has been officially denied."[8]

---

8.   "Since becoming a journalist I have often heard the advice to 'believe nothing until it has been officially denied.'" Claud Cockburn, *I, Claud . . . : The Autobiography of Claud Cockburn* (New York: Penguin, 1967), 97.

5

Situation in the Basque Country

Since the abolition of the Basque laws at the end of the Second Carlist Wars in 1876, various Basque political forces had claimed the devolution of the historical rights of the Basque people. After the proclamation of the Spanish Republic in 1932, two projects of statute of autonomy promoted by the Basque Nationalist Party (EAJ-PNV) and Basque Nationalist Action (ANV) were rejected at the Spanish parliament. Finally, after the approval of the statute of autonomy on October 6, 1936, Jose A. Agirre became the Lehendakari or president of the Basque Government and took his oath under the tree of Gernika one day later. A government of democratic concentration was formed with members of all the democratic parties opposed to the coup led by Agirre's political party, EAJ-PNV.

*Lehendakari Jose A. Agirre taking the
oath under the tree of Gernika.*

Despite not being part of the Popular Front
and being a Catholic party, EAJ-PNV was firm-
ly positioned itself in opposition to the uprising
since there was nothing on the political or reli-
gious level that linked the Basque nationalists
with the rebels. In fact, one day after the coup
d'etat, on July 19 at dawn, the Basque deputies
Manuel Irujo and Joxemari Lasarte announced
on the radio that the EAJ-PNV would remain
on the side of the Republic without abandon-
ing its political goals, among them the fight
for the independence of the Basque Country.
The National Movement led by General Franco
represented totalitarianism against the democratic republicanism of the Basque nationalists;
political centralism versus the proclamation of
the political and cultural rights of the Basque

people; and, finally, a hierarchical and doctrinaire Catholicism, very far from the Christian-democrat ideology of Jacques Maritain that the Basque nationalists professed. In short, the Basque nationalists confronted the coup leaders because they were Christians and Catholics, because they were democrats, and because they were Basque nationalists.

The confrontation was inevitable and the first aerial attack on Basque soil, the bombardment of Otxandio, took place on July 22, just four days after the military uprising was proclaimed and three days after the Basque nationalist deputies Irujo and Lasarte announced by radio from Donostia (San Sebastián in Spanish) the frontal refusal of the Basque nationalists to the ideological positions and the military strategy of the conspirators.

However, the political and military situation that the nascent Basque government was facing was extremely difficult. Having occupied Donostia, by October 1936 the troops of General Emilio Mola controlled Araba and Navarre and were advancing toward Bilbao. By the end of September the Basque Country had suffered 150 bombing operations and the death toll—especially among civilians—already rose to the hundreds.

6

Atrocities

From the beginning of the war the Francoist troops committed atrocities in the Basque Country. This was announced by General Emilio Mola during a meeting with mayors from the area of Iruñea-Pamplona as early as July 19, 1936, just one day after the uprising: "We must spread terror . . . , we have to create the impression of mastery by eliminating without scruple or hesitation all those who do not think like us. There can be no cowardice. If we vacillate for one moment and fail to proceed with the greatest determination, we will not win."[1] And he roared, "in this trance of war I have already decided the all-out war. As for the military who have not joined our Movement, throw them out

---

1.   Juan Iturralde [pseud. Juan Jose Usabiaga Irazustabarrena], *El catolicismo y la cruzada de Franco*, (Vienna: EGI Indarra, 1960), vol. 2, 88.

and take their pay from them. Those who have taken weapons against us, against the army, shoot them. If I see my father in the opposite ranks, I would shoot him."[2]

José M. Iribarren, Mola's secretary, wrote in his memoirs that the general used to say about six months after the coup that "a year ago I would have trembled to sign a death sentence. I could have not slept with grief. Today I sign three and four every day for the auditor and I feel so calm! . . ." Iribarren wrote by hand in the book, "they were more (than three or four executions a day)."[3]

In those territories controlled by the Francoists since the beginning of the war, numerous executive arrests, imprisonments, and executions happened since July 1936. The registry of persons executed in Navarre, the vast majority of them civilians, amounts to 3,452 dead in a territory that in 1936 did not reach 350,000 inhabitants. The executions became a routine activity to accompany war actions. Iribarren tells an anecdote about the effect of the numerous executions in society under the heading "children's game": "I went to the dike. I was shocked by the game that some kids were playing. Two of them went with toy shotguns.

---

2.   Alberto Reig Tapia, *Ideología e historia: Sobre la represión franquista y la guerra civil*, (Madrid: Akal, 1986), 146.

3.   José María Iribarren, *Con el general Mola: Escenas y aspectos inéditos de la Guerra Civil*, (Zaragoza: Librería General, 1937), 245.

General Emilio Mola.

The others took another prisoner and led him in front of the armed ones. They shouted to the prisoner: 'Long live Spain! Long live Spain!' and as the prisoner did not answer (the game was not to answer), and then they pointed their shotguns at him and they played the execution."[4]

The bodies of the people executed were initially thrown into the river or simply left at the place of execution. However, very soon the bodies started to be buried or deposited in chasms

---

4. These events occurred nearby Somosierra, about twenty kilometers north of Buitrago de Lozoya. In Iribarren, *Con el general Mola*, 191.

*Seminarians posing with guns in the
bullring in Pamplona.*

in order to make them disappear, which has
made it very difficult to quantify the deaths
today. In ten years of work, the Nafarroako
Fusilatuen Senitartekoen Elkartea/Asociación
de Familiares de Fusilados, Asesinados y
Desaparecidos en Navarra en 1936 (Association
of Relatives of Victims in Navarre of 1936) has
found a total of 217 bodies and has delivered
88 remains found in 46 pits to their families.[5]
Such is the case of the victims found in 2012 in
Urbasa, an isolated area where sometimes dead
cattle had been thrown. The bodies of ten adults
(possibly nine men and one woman) were found

---

5.   "Aumentan a diez los cadáveres de la Guerra Civil recu-
     perados en la sima El Raso, en la sierra de Urbasa," Na-
     barralde, Hemeroteca, April 2, 2013. See www.nabarralde.
     com (2015).

along with the remains of a horse, a sheep, a pig, and three dogs. As the forensic doctor Francisco Etxeberria explained, "the remains showed obvious signs of a violent death. In two of the skulls the shot of a small caliber pistol with an inlet and outlet hole could be seen."[6] Seven of the victims died as a result of a single pistol shot in the skull; the remaining three would die only after they were administered the coup of grace. In order to make the bodies disappear, they were thrown into the twenty-meter deep chasm where a grenade that did not explode was thrown. As Etxeberria relates, human remains were found next to dog bones. The first ones were gnawed while the second ones did not show notches. Apparently, the executioners introduced several dogs into the chasm that ate the bodies of the victims and later died of hunger. In some cases, in order to avoid recognition of the remains the head of those executed was crushed with a vehicle to disfigure the faces. In other cases the bodies were incinerated.

At present, and in the absence of further research work, several authors consider that the number of fatalities of the judicial and extrajudicial executions of the regime in the Basque Country—with a population in 1930 of 1,237,593 inhabitants—amounts to a total of between 5,000 and 8,000 people, of which

---

6. Garikoitz, Montañés, "El Raso, de matadero a sepultura 'digna,'" *El Diario*, July 1, 2015. See www.aranzadi.eus (2015)

more than half were executed in Navarra. This represents a rate of executions of between 4 percent and 6.5 percent.[7]

With regard to the hearing of cases and the execution of sentences, there are several interesting testimonies that shed light on these facts. The victims of these trials and the subsequent executions were tried as members of a group, so they were judged and executed en masse and not individually, something typical in episodes of genocide. The report *The Basque Country under the Franco regime* written by the Basque Government gathers information about these processes:

> A few days after the occupation of Bilbao, what we may call Franco's "legal justice" began to take place intensely. Several permanent military tribunals tried a large number of people on a daily basis. Even if the action of the "organized justice" was more extensive in Bizkaia than in Gipuzkoa, and the performance of the "checas" [unofficial executions] and "uncontrolled" executions was also minor, the repressive nature of justice in Bizkaia was not less cruel if we look at the arbitrary and the absurd criterion with which military

---

7.   Xabier Irujo, *Genocidio en Euskal Herria* (Iruñea-Pamplona: Nabarralde, 2015), 150.

tribunals acted. The trials—with rare exceptions—were, and still are, global. That is to say, each one of them saw cases where detainees who did not even know each other were tried and they were accused and found responsible for the most different causes. Sometimes, there were ten; others, twenty; frequently, fifty people without any relationship among them were judged in a single trial. Its development was purely 'mechanical', of ritual. The prosecutor read the accusation—based not on facts or on the actual performance of the defendants, but on the allegations that, naturally, were unfavorable to them—and the court, in general, always approved the penalties proposed by the prosecutor.

The law did not exist in practice. Defenders were appointed but in most cases they did not even meet with the defendants, and the defendants did not even know who was going to defend them. Their trial work was without any preparation, of course, limited to fulfill the assignment as quickly as possible and without any interest or enthusiasm. There have been many cases in which the defender complied with the request of the prosecutor, although this would entail an irreparable harm to their defendants.

The sentences were consistent with the false accusations and the code of military justice applied rigorously in all cases. The simplest fact, for instance having been the hairdresser of a Basque battalion, the administrative assistance or clerk in a dependency of the Basque Government or having been affiliated to an anti-Franco political party, was considered a crime of "rebellion." And death penalty or life imprisonment applied in a high percentage of the cases."[8]

For example, the report mentions the 323 judgments for various reasons issued in the military tribunals held in Bilbao during the fifteen days of the months of July and August 1937, all of them published in the newspaper *La Gaceta del Norte*. In this period an average of twenty-one sentences were issued daily, 64.39 percent of them being death or sentences of more than twenty years of imprisonment. Only 4.6 percent of the accused were ever acquitted.[9]

More than 150,000 people escaped into exile (12 percent of the total Basque population), including 32,000 underage children who had

---

8.   *Euzkadi bajo el régimen de Franco: La represión en Bizkaia*, Archivo del Nacionalismo Vasco, Basterra 03 01, GE-545-1.

9.   Ibid.

to face exile without their parents (20 percent of the minor population in the area controlled by the Government of Euskadi). Most of them never returned to their homes.[10]

The Basque clergy was also subject to repression. There were at least seventeen Basque priests executed by the regime on Basque soil, all of them extra-judicially executed. The military judge Ramiro Llamas expressed at the hearing in Donostia: "That we have shot sixteen priests? We'll shot 160." And he used to repeat also that any Basque nationalist priest who came to his hands "would be dispatched by him immediately."[11] A large percentage of the Basque clergy was purged, imprisoned and many suffered exile.

Apart from extrajudicial killings, prison sentences and exile, the range of atrocities of the Franco regime was varied. Torture was common practice in the barracks and prisons of the military government until the death of the dictator in 1975. The regime also executed property embargoes, imposed fines of all kinds, and, under article three of the proclamation of July 28, 1937, extending to the entire territory

10. Euskadiko Artxibo Historikoa, I-501/4-7. In a note of the delegation of the Basque government in London dated March 17, 1939 the figure of 150,000 exiles is also registered. Basque National Archive-Euskadiko Artxibo Historikoa, I-502/4-7.

11. Mateo Múgica, *Imperativos de mi conciencia: Carta abierta al presbítero D. José Miguel de Barandiarán* (Buenos Aires: Liga de Amigos de los Vascos, [1945?]).

of the state the state of war previously declared in certain provinces, purged each and every one of the public administration's servants, with special attention to teachers, who could only recover their jobs if they proved to be "support-ers of the regime" by a committee composed in most cases by an army officer and the local par-ish priest.[12]

---

12.   Proclamation of July 28, 1937, extending to the entire territory of the state the state of war previously declared in certain provinces [Bando haciendo extensivo a todo el territorio nacional el estado de guerra declarado ya en determinadas provincias]. Boletín Oficial de la Junta de Defensa Nacional de España, No. 3, July 30, 1936, pp. 9-10.

7

A Brutal War

As for the air force, Richthofen agreed with Colonel Juan Vigón, Chief of Staff of the Francoist troops at the Basque front, that the air units would attack enemy positions, local reserves, and other sectors "without taking into consideration civilian casualties."[1]

Just four days after the coup d'etat, on July 22, 1936, two ground attack aircraft Breguet Br.19 departing from the Recajo airfield, located about ten kilometers east of Logroño, appeared over Otxandio a small town in Bizkaia of less than 1,400 inhabitants. "It was the fourth day of the Francoist military uprising. People in town were celebrating the festival of the patron saint when at about nine o'clock in the morning some planes flying at regular height, rather

1. Klaus A. Maier, *Guernica. La intervención alemana en España y el "caso Guernica,"* (Madrid: Sedmay, 1976), 52.

According to the Francoist Propaganda the coup d'état and the subsequent war was a struggle against the infidels, a Saintly Crusade.

low, as they almost touched the church tower flew over the town. They circled the town several times. The pilots saluted with their hands to the people who contemplated and cheered them fascinated."[2] Carmelo Bernaola, witness of the bombing, corroborated that flying at the height of the bell tower of Santa Marina, the pilots attracted by gestures to a large number of children who, as had happened in previous days, waited

2.   Xabier Irujo, "El bombardeo de Otxandio según el general Salas," *Deia*, July 18, 2015, 18–19.

for a rain of pamphlets shouting "papelak die!, papelak die!" ("Leaflets, leaflets!")

After making several circles at about seventy meters of altitude, they bombed and machine-gunned the Andikona square where a large number of children had gathered. Although the minors were unaware of the meaning of war and did not know what a terror bombardment consisted of, at this point the pilots were well aware that the victims were civilians because they saw them perfectly. The aerial attack continued for about twenty-five minutes, executing repeated passes and throwing all the bombs they carried.

José A. Maurolagoitia, doctor of Otxandio, one of the first people to arrive to the place after the bombing, described what he saw:

> I went out to the street heading to Andicona square. Due to the nature of my profession I have seen painful episodes, but nothing as terrible as the vision of Andicona. It was not the ramshackle roofs, nor the downed power lines. It was something more serious and more terrible; it was human pain. People torn apart, children mutilated, women beheaded. The cries of the peasants in Basque begging me to cure them; it was the torrent of blood that ran toward the water of the little fountain that rises in the middle

of the square. I asked for help, which was given to me urgently and caringly. With sheets, with strips of sheets, I proceeded to perform urgent cures. There were some, many, who unfortunately did not need anything. They had perished by the barbarous shrapnel produced by the many bombs that were dropped twice. Other boys and girls, with hanging limbs, came to me asking for their lives in Basque and I still have that stuck in my heart.[3]

Various testimonies corroborate doctor Maurolagoitia's statement: "When the planes left, we passed through the place of the bombing. Unable to recognize family members, badly disfigured, we saw dead bodies crushed against the wall, some cut off at the waist, others without heads."[4] The correspondent of the Euzkadi newspaper also wrote: "Large pools of blood that no one has bothered to clean up and several human remains: a piece of head, fingers, brain tissue stuck to the stones and the fountain give a macabre impression to a place that in itself is joyful and cheerful."[5]

The first bombing of Otxandio claimed sixty-one dead, forty-five of the victims were civilians, nine were soldiers, and there is no

3.   Ibid.

4.   Ibid.

5.   Ibid.

information about the rest. That is, at least 73.77 percent of the victims were civilians and twenty-four were minors, 39 percent of the total. Sixteen of the dead were less than ten years old (26 percent).[6] The reporter of the newspaper *Euzkadi* expressed that Sabina Oianguren had a lifeless gaze. In half an hour she had lost her husband, Emeterio Garces, and four of her five children: Pedro, Juan Manuel, Teodoro, and Maria Jesus. The oldest was thirteen years of age.

This was the first aerial bombardment on Basque soil of the war, and in the history of the Basque Country.

---

6.   Zigor Olabarria, *Gerra Zibila Otxandion* (Donostia-San Sebastián: Eusko Ikaskuntza, 2011), 79 and 81.

8

Terror Bombing Campaign

On April 26, 1937, the rebel air force had executed more than six hundred bombing operations on Basque soil. But, despite the overwhelming air superiority, after a month of campaign, the Francoist troops only managed to advance to Elorrio from the south (10 kilometers) and had not been able to advance from the east: an average advance of just 0.4 kilometers per day. The scarce material results of the offensive caused the intensification of the bombardments and the multiplication of aerial attacks on urban nuclei in order to break the morale of its defenders and, as Richthofen and Vigón agreed, the German, Italian, and Spanish air units attacked "without consideration of the civil population."

If at the beginning of April the aerial bombardments were circumscribed to an average of ten bombing and ground attacks per day, between April 22 and 26, up to 15.6 operations were registered every day. In April about 250 bombing operations were recorded, in May the number reached 300. The spring offensive closed on August 18 with a terrifying balance of more than 650 rebel bombing operations on Basque soil. Richthofen notably increased the number of airplanes in flight and the total tonnage of bombs thrown per day and improved the destructive capacity of them by producing new mixtures of explosive and incendiary bombs.

More than forty bombers and sixty fighters flew practically every day over the Basque soil between March 31 and June 19, 1937, performing several sorties a day. War began every day at eight in the morning with a heavy artillery fire over the Basque frontline positions that were usually located at strategic points in the mountains. Around nine o'clock in the morning the first air attack took place, usually carried out by a units of the Spanish rebel air force, a bombing unit of the Condor Legion, and the ground attack aircraft Heinkel He 51s supported by the Heinkel He 45 and Heinkel He 70 reconnaissance planes that also strafed land positions. After fifty minutes of intense aerial bombardment and machine-gunning, there was a second attack by the rebel artillery in collaboration with the 88 mm FlaK 18 anti-aircraft guns of the Condor Legion (which, given the total absence of Republican aircraft, served throughout the campaign as pieces of ground artillery) followed by a bombing attack carried out by rebel planes. At about two o'clock in the afternoon the procedure was repeated until between seven and eleven air strikes were executed on the same position. Several Basque cities and towns were also bombed on a daily basis, mostly in the afternoon. One hour before dusk, the troops received the order to advance over the shelled positions.[1]

As Richthofen wrote in his diary, the bombing campaign of the spring of 1937 on the Basque front had a double moral and material effect on the Basque militias. On the one hand, rebel aviation bombarded and relentlessly machine-gunned the positions of the front and, on the other hand, the morale of the Basque people was bombarded by the systematic, daily attack of the localities located far from the front, and by the air machine-gunning of the population that passed by roads far from the front.[2] According to the German colonel, the whole weight of the struggle fell on the Condor Legion, which depressed the enemy morally by constantly hammering their positions and the rearguard. Only after having intensely bombarded these positions did the infantry advance. Gernika represented the epitome of terror bombing but the

---

1.   Xabier Irujo, "Bonbaketa kanpaina Enkarterrin," in Javier Barrio, et al., eds., *"Itxaropena iñoiz ez da galtzen": Encartaciones. 1937: Los últimos meses de la guerra civil en Euskadi* (Bilbao: Bizkaiko Batzar Nagusiak, 2017), 97–98.

2.   Maier, *Guernica*, 130.

Basque Country suffered a total of more than 1,100 bombing operations between July 22, 1936 and August 18, 1937, when the last bombardment on Basque soil was recorded.

Bombing of Durango by Italian planes on March 31, 1937.

There are very few municipalities in Bizkaia that were not repeatedly bombarded. In view of the data we have today, with a total record of fifty-six bombings, Legutio was together with Bilbao the most bombed population during the war. Markina and Zornotza suffered forty bombing operations, Zigoiti thirty-three, Mungia thirty-two, Bermeo twenty-nine, Galdakao twenty-seven; Eibar, Otxandio, and Larrabetzu twenty-five, Irun and Leioa twenty-three; Elorrio, Lemoa, and Barakaldo twenty-two; Arrasate and the positions of their municipality in Santa Marina , Udala, and Kurtze Txiki were bombarded up to twenty-one times;

Durango, Sondika, and Donostia eighteen (of these last eight naval); Dima and Getxo fourteen, Lezama and Zeanuri fifteen; Ubide fourteen; Arrigorriaga, Lekeitio, Ugao-Miravalles, and Zuia thirteen, Abadiño twelve, the positions of Bergara, Ondarroa, Elgoibar, and Mañaria eleven, the list continues endlessly. And most of these cities were open cities with no military interest.[3]

An Italian bomber Savoia Marchetti
SM.81.

Virtually every morning Richthofen rode to the top of a hill from where he watched the shelling of the Basque positions in the front taking notes in order to perfect the launch of the bombs and find ways to better coordinate ground operations with aerial bombardments on the front lines. In the afternoons,

3. Irujo, "Bonbaketa kanpaina Enkarterrin," 97-98.

he examined the ruins of the cities and towns that had been captured by the rebels in order to observe and measure the degree of destruction obtained and to improve the effects of the aerial raids. He studied, developed, and applied techniques to improve aerial bombardment and very soon discovered that the prolongation of the bombings in time dramatically increased their destructive potential. It was preferable to launch sixty tons of bombs in half an hour than to do it in two minutes as he had tried on April 4 on the summit of Mount Motxotegi, a small 799-meter summit that in his own words he "turned into a horrible sea of flames and smoke."[4] He sometimes recorded his observations in his diary, such as on April 4 when he wrote: "I have gone to Ochandiano [Otxandio]. Great effects of the bombing, and of the fighters [Heinkel He 51 and Messerschmitt Bf 109] and of the A/8 [Heinkel He 70 and Heinkel He 45 aircraft of the reconnaissance squadrons]. Everywhere people dead and mutilated, heavy trucks, carrying part of their ammunition, in pieces. Ochandiano very destroyed, with many corpses."[5]

---

4.   Richthofen's diary entry of April 4, 1937. In Maier, *Guernica*, 103–4.

5.   Ibid., 104.

9

The Naval Blockade

Those people who escaped from the Francoist side in different parts of the Basque Country sought refuge in Bilbao. At the end of April 1937 Bilbao sheltered 150,000 people without homes, without means and, in many cases, without contact with their loved ones in the areas occupied by the rebels.

In March of 1937 Franco ordered the naval blockade of Bilbao to accelerate the city's fall by starvation. Following these instructions, on April 6 the rebel ship *Cervera* tried to prevent the access to Bilbao of the British merchant ship *Thorpehall*, which provoked the intervention of several ships of the British Navy. After a tense encounter, the Francoist ships withdrew and the merchant ship entered Bilbao but the British government warned the British ship owners that their vessels were in danger of being attacked. The rumor that the rebels had placed mines in Basque waters also circulated in London.

But a deed came to change the course of events. On April 20, William H. Roberts, captain of the *Seven Seas Spray*, threw himself into the sea in an effort to break the naval siege of Bilbao. In waters controlled by rebel vessels, without any protection and after being warned by the British government that he was acting on his own, Roberts placed his daughter Fifi on the keel of his ship and entered the port of Bilbao with his cargo of sugar, flour, lentils, and barrels of cognac: "I did not see a damned rebel warship nor a single mine"[1] were his words to the media, and so the blockade ceased.[2]

But although maritime shipments alleviated hunger for a few days, they were not enough, so the Basque Government's trade and supply department issued an order on January 30, 1937, under which the city councils had to organize weekly markets and "facilitate and recommend the greatest concurrence" of farmers and consumers to these markets in different cities and towns in the area controlled by the Basque

---

1. "Foreign News: Welsh Basques," *Time*, May 3, 1937.

2. *Parliamentary Debates*, 5th ser., vol. 323, House of Commons, Official Report, 2nd sess., 37th Parliament of the United Kingdom of Great Britain and Northern Ireland, 7th vol., sess. 1936–1937, His Majesty's Stationery Office, London, 1937, col. 11.

Government.[3] The order specified that the city councils had to overcome as many difficulties as they might find in order to comply with the supply of food in the corresponding municipal term.[4] And that is why the Basque Government organized up to seven special trains to facilitate transportation to Gernika that Monday, April 26, 1937. As Uxua Madariaga expressed, buses from different parts of Bizkaia arrived in Gernika full of people who came looking for food and livestock, and also to have fun. The trains also came full of people from Bilbao and surrounding areas."[5]

3.   Acta de la Reunión de Alcaldes del Distrito de Gernika, February 24, 1937.

4.   Acta de constitución de la Comisión Permanente del Distrito de Guernica y Bases por las que ha de regirse para el abastecimiento de los pueblos, February 15, 1937. BFA, Busturia 0056/030.

5.   Testimony of Uxua Makazaga. In William Smallwood, *The Day Guernica Was Bombed* (Gernika: Gernika-Lumoko udala, 2012), 26.

10

Anti-Aircraft Shelters

In the view of these indiscriminate aerial attacks, the mayor of Gernika Jose Labauria ordered the municipal architect Castor Uriarte to build a series of shelters in accordance with provisions the Basque Government had made public. Located in strategic areas of the town, there were a total of between twelve and sixteen shelters (six of them unfinished) public and private of different sizes with a capacity for three thousand people.

> The refuges were all built about the same. Pine logs, 2½ meters tall and about 35 centimeters in diameter, were used as pillars. Other logs of the same diameter were used as ceiling beams. Over the top of the logs we placed five millimeter steel sheets and

*Civilians running to the shelters during a
raid against Bilbao.*

two layers of sand bags over them. In
some cases, for example in the city hall
and the Conde Arana Mansion, this
construction was done in the first floor
or basement of a building that was
well constructed and made of stone.
But we used other places. For example, the narrow Calle Santa Maria in
the center of the town, between Arte
Calle and Barren Calle, was completely covered and used as a single refuge.
It was about 40 meters long and had
entrances from both streets. In effect
it was just a covered street . . .The safest refuges were on the west side of
the Plaza de la Unión. The wall on this
side of the Plaza is against a hillside.
We simply dug four cave-like refuges

back into the hill. They were about 10 meters deep. A visitor can still see the outline of the half-elliptical doorways that have since been filled in. These four refuges were intended for the people in the area of the market.[1]

Bomb deposit of the rebel army.

The shelters built by Uriarte would have sufficed considering that Gernika, an open city, should never have been bombed. But nobody expected an attack of the dimensions of that of April 26. As experience had shown, not even fortified refuges with two-meter cement walls could withstand the direct impact of a 250 kilos bomb. A 250-kilogram bomb with a delay fuse could pierce an old six-story limestone building and up to five floors in a reinforced concrete house, "penetrating the buildings like

---

1.   Testimony of Castor Uriarte. In Smallwood, *The Day Guernica Was Bombed*, 29.

knives." When exploding at ground level, the whole building collapsed, so that those who did not die because of the explosion or subsequent fire would die slowly, buried alive under tons of rubble.

The experience in the shelters was very traumatic and the three-and-a-half hours of bombing became eternal. Once inside, it was practically impossible to move due to over-crowding. Without air because of the dust and the smoke, the feeling of suffocation was terrible, amplified by heat and thirst. At the same time, the explosions generated a sharp pain in the ears and the expansive waves of the detonations caused strong vibrations in the structures that in turn generated contagious anguish and scenes of panic.

11

Upset of the Rebel Leaders

In the light of the slow advance of the rebel troops in Bizkaia, enemies of Minister Hermann Göring in Berlin and General Emilio Mola in Salamanca circulated the rumor that Bilbao was not going to fall. And, just as Hugo Sperrle was being pressured from Berlin by Göring, Ettore Bastico was being pressured by Mussolini from Rome who urgently needed a quick victory on the Basque front to recover from the disaster of the Italian troops in Guadalajara in March 1937.

The German and Italian commanders blamed Mola for the slowness of the advance, disqualifying him before Franco. Mola exonerated himself by explaining to Richthofen that his plan was to destroy the industry of Bizkaia and turn the Basque Country into a rural area in order to root out Basque nationalism that was based—according to him—on the wealth of Basque industry. Therefore the advance must be slow and the destruction of the Basque industrial wealth absolute in order to "clean up Spain" and put an end to the Basque separatism.

As a consequence of all the above, the campaign of terror bombings was accentuated and General Mola ordered the launching of the airplanes of leaflets announcing the total destruction of Bizkaia: "I have decided to quickly end the war in the North of Spain. Those who are not perpetrators of murders and lay down their weapons or surrender will be respected in life and wealth. If your submission is not immediate I will raze Bizkaia to the ground starting with the war industries. I have plenty of means for this. General Emilio Mola."[1]

Göring also had a great personal interest in the bombing campaign since he wanted to convince Hitler that the air force was his best weapon and, therefore, he had to prove to the latter that the Luftwaffe was capable of actions that were not within the reach of the infantry or the navy, for example, to reduce to ashes urban nuclei located far from the front line in record time. Having achieved this, he would be in a position to convince Hitler that he should invest in the air force and that the person in command

---

1.   Leaflet to be thrown from the airplanes. See reproduction of the original in Xabier Irujo, *El Gernika de Richthofen: Un ensayo de bombardeo de terror* (Gernika: Gernikako Bakearen Museoa Fundazioa/Gernika-Lumoko Udala, 2012), 308.

of the Luftwaffe should therefore become the second strong man of the Reich.

Hitler's birthday, April 20, was one of the three most important festivities in Nazi Germany. Göring intended to offer a bombardment as a gift to the Führer, as he would on April 20, 1940 in Namsos, on April 20, 1941 in Athens, on April 19, 1941 in Plymouth and London (a thousand tons of explosive and 153,000 incendiaries with a balance of 1,200 deaths), on April 20, 1942 in Malta, and, on April 19, 1944 in London: the most massive and devastating bombings of the Luftwaffe occurred on the occasion of Hitler's birthdays. However, on Monday, April 19, Gernika could not be bombed due to the bad weather, and the bombing was postponed to the next market day, Monday April 26.

12

Seven Reasons to Bomb Gernika

There were seven main reasons why Gernika was chosen for the site of this massive terror bombing.

1. Gernika had an adequate size. The town was large enough to be a military objective and small enough to be destroyed in its entirety with the number of aircraft and the quantity and quality of the explosives available to the rebels in April 1937.

2. The town was about twenty-three kilometers from the front line, so it could be occupied a few days after the attack, before the International Committee of the Red Cross, the press, or other international

organizations could report, take photographs, or get any other type of physical evidence of the bombing.

3. The villa was completely defenseless and did not have anti-aircraft batteries.

4. Most of the buildings in the town were stuck to one another in closed blocks, separated by narrow streets, and had internal wooden structures, which would prove the usefulness and destructive capacity of the new German incendiary bombs that would be thrown by the thousands after the explosive bombs of 250 kilos.

5. Gernika was one of the capitals of district in wartime and the front in the Markina sector depended on its weekly market and its three hospitals. The destruction of these resources would spell disaster for the front at Markina.

6. Gernika had not been bombed before. Richthofen needed to experiment and measure the results of his raids on the ground, but since most of the population centers were being bombarded by German, Italian, and Spanish units, it was difficult to know the effect that the attacks of the Luftwaffe units had had in these

objectives. Gernika was suitable for a war experiment.

7. Gernika, seat of the oak that symbolizes representative democracy and Basque freedom, a place venerated by the Basque people, was an ideal target to break the morale of the Basque troops, which would be required to surrender the day after the bombing under the threat of repeating these attacks against other Basque cities. It was not the first time that Gernika had become the target of the wrath of generals of different colors. Under the slogan of the Liberal Party "Ancient Laws and Petrol," General Baldomero Espartero had already ordered in 1835, one hundred years before the bombing, to burn the oak of Gernika, the Parliament of Bizkaia and the whole town, and place an inscription on its ruins in which it was read: "Here was Gernika."[1] The Gernikako arbola by Jose M. Iparragirre, a poem composed in 1853, is still considered by many Basques the unofficial anthem of the Basque Country and the oak

---

1. José Francisco Isla, *Compendio de la historia de España* (Madrid: Compañía General de Impresores y Libreros, 1845), 454.

itself, the symbol of the freedoms and democratic virtues of the nation. Therefore, it was foreseeable that the attack was going to have a strong impact on the Basque society. On the other hand, "liberties and democracy" were two of the "errors" that Franco and Mola sought to eradicate.

13

Preparations for the Bombing of Gernika

Although shipments of troops and war material in support of the rebels began to be sent at the end of July, the Condor Legion would not be set until November 6, 1936. The total number of German "volunteers" would amount to twenty thousand in the whole war, but never exceeded six to eight thousand men at the same time in the theater of operations. The Condor Legion would not operate in the Basque Country until the spring offensive of 1937.

At the end of February 1937 the Italian military unit, called Corpo Truppe Volontarie (CTV), was composed of some fifty thousand men under General Mario Roatta. Unlike the Condor Legion, the Italian units were composed primarily of infantry units, some of them armored. The air force of this expeditionary army, known as Aviazione Legionaria, was

Gernika before the bombing.

composed of about five thousand men. As in the case of the Condor Legion, the Italian air units would not act decisively in Basque soil until the spring offensive of 1937.

The German, Italian, and Spanish units would act during the 1937 spring campaign in the Basque Country under the command of General Franco but coordinated by Richthofen in close cooperation with Colonel Juan Vigón, chief of staff of the rebel land units in the Basque Country. As mentioned, the rebel command had 160 German and Italian planes destined to the Basque front plus an unknown number of aircraft of the Spanish rebel air force. To deal with this air force, the Basque government had only eight Polikarpov I-15 fighter planes stationed at the Lamiako airfield in early April. By the end of the month, there was hardly any republican aircraft left in flight.[1]

The data available indicate that between fifty-nine and sixty-two aircraft took part in the bombing of Gernika: between twenty-seven and thirty bombers and thirty-two fighters and ground attack aircraft, some of which carried out more than one sortie over Gernika. This represented 20 percent of the rebel aviation in the whole of the Iberian Peninsula in April 1937.[2] The participation of Heinkel He 45 and Heinkel He 70 reconnaissance aircraft from the Lasarte and Vitoria-Gasteiz airports in observation work has been also documented. These aircraft routinely operated as ground attack aircraft, machine-gunning and bombarding with ten- and fifty-kilogram bombs.

---

1.   Report No. 31 from Henry Chilton, Ambassador of Great Britain, to the air intelligence services. April 11, 1937. Kew Archives, HW 22/1.

2.   Irujo, *El Gernika de Richthofen*, 151.

Model	Origen	Use	No.	Unit	Air base
Junker Ju 52	German	Bomber	21	K/88	Burgos
Heinkel He 111	German	Bomber	2	VB/88	Burgos
Dornier Do 17	German	Bomber	1	VB/88	Burgos
Savoia-Marchetti SM.79	Italian	Bomber	3/6	E-280	Soria
Heinkel He 51	German	Ground attack	12	J/88	Vitoria-Gasteiz
Messerschmitt Bf 109	German	Fighter	7	J/88	Vitoria-Gasteiz
Fiat Cr.32	Italian	Fighter	13	3-26	Vitoria-Gasteiz

Type and number of airplanes used in the attack

14

A Military Experiment and a Terror Bombing

Gernika was an open city, that is, it was not defended nor was it a center for supplying the Basque troops at the front since the weekly market place was an entirely civilian market place. There were no headquarters in the town either. Some of the convents in Gernika were equipped for the repose of the troops or for the physical recovery of wounded soldiers but not to organize war operations.

Gernika was bombarded to test the new method of high-density "Koppelwurf" bombing by increasing the number of explosive and incendiary bombs dropped within a condensed area, called an "air corral." The high mortality rate of the bombing of Gernika is explained by the fact that approximately forty tons of bombs were launched in a space of 0.13 square kilomters where between ten and twelve thosuand people

were concentrated, most of them civilians without military knowledge, easy targets for the
airplanes.

In order to hide the true intention of the
bombing, Richthofen alleged in his diary that
the objective of the attack on Gernika had
been to destroy "the bridge and the road" to
Errenteria "passage point of the enemy retreat."[1] That is, according to Richthofen the
Basque troops fighting on the fronts of Elgeta,
Eibar, and Markina would retire to Bilbao
through Gernika and by blowing up the bridge
at Errenteria the battalions of Basque troops
would be trapped when they could not cross the
Oka River.

This hypothesis, which some authors still
maintain, has no support whatsoever. In the first
place, the Basque troops would never have retreated to Bilbao through Gernika but through
Durango and Zornotza, which is the main road
linking the front with Bilbao. Anyone who
looks at a map of the area can see that retreating from Eibar to Gernika and then accessing
Bilbao through Bermeo is completely illogical.
In addition, retreating through Gernika would
have meant endangering the southwest sector
of the front, leaving Zornotza fully exposed to
the advance of rebel troops. In fact, as expressed
by the chief of staff of the Basque army Sabin
Apraiz, the troops were ordered not to retreat

---

1.   Richthofen's diary entry of April 26, 1937. In Maier,
      Guernica, 121.

through Gernika.² And they did not.

Apart from this, it is simply absurd to suppose that infantry troops scarcely mechanized and retreating on foot, can be stopped by blowing up a single bridge twenty meters long and ten wide on the Oka River, which barely reaches a meter and a half deep. The Oka River was easily forded by infantry units at many points. Moreover, Richthofen never ordered an attack on the railroad between Gernika and Zornotza, which was one of the two main communication routes between Gernika and Bilbao through the south. In fact, the evacuation of the population that survived the bombing was carried out by seven trains, following the Gernika-Zornotza-Bilbao route.

It is even more absurd to believe that the destruction of a twenty by ten meter bridge required the participation of twenty-seven bombers and thirty-two fighters and ground attack aircraft for three-and-a-half hours and the launching of between thirty-one and forty-six tons of bombs. It is even more absurd to think that explosive bombs with delayed effect fuses were necessary to carry out the destruction of a bridge whose surface is totally flat and, in short, even more absurd to believe that the destruction of the bridge required the

---

2. Luis M. Jiménez de Aberasturi and Juan C. Jiménez de Aberasturi, *La guerra en Euskadi* (Donostia-San Sebastián: Txertoa, 2007), 68. See also Vicente Talón, *El holocausto de Guernica* (Barcelona: Plaza & Janés, 1987), 40.

use of thousands of incendiary bombs and the aerial machine-gunning of civilians for hours. As the commander of one of Junkers Ju 52's squadrons that bombarded Gernika, Erhart K. Dellmensingen ironically put it, "when I was denied permission to modify the cargo [and retire the incendiary bombs] I said: well, let's suppose they are wooden bridges."[3]

As Pete Cenarrusa, a dive bomber pilot and instructor of dive bomber pilots in World War II said after having studied the location and dimensions of the Errenteria bridge and studied the structure of the old one, a static objective like that one could perfectly be reached with a single bomb of 250 kilos by means of a single dive bomber.[4] Moreover, Richthofen used all the available airplanes in the aerodromes destined to the Basque front except four: the four dive bombers Henschell Hs123 that he had available in the aerodrome of Vitoria-Gasteiz, a hardly twenty-minute flight from Gernika.[5]

Finally, Cenarrusa expressed that if these men had flown at their orders, after throwing approximately forty tons of bombs on a twenty

3.   *Auswertung Rügen. Heft 2, Führung, Abschnitte IV bis VI*, file RL 7/57b. Ángel Viñas, "Epílogo [a la nueva edición de la obra de Herbert Southworth sobre el bombardeo de Gernika]," manuscript, 58.

4.   Interviews with Pete T. Cenarrusa in his house in Boise, ID on Monday, April 18 2010 and Thursday, November 11 2010.

5.   Pietro Pinna, *Relazioni del General Pinna*, Salamanca, abril 17, 1937. USAM, Busta 104, Fascicolo 8, p. 30, anexo 1.

meter bridge for three and a half hours without even touching it, they would not have touched a plane for the rest of the war, and Richthofen would have been immediately dismissed for incompetence.

It is obvious that Richthofen lied and that he tried to disguise a terror bombing as a strategic one alleging that his intention was to destroy the Errenteria Bridge and cut off the withdrawal of the Basque battalions that never retreated through Gernika. Quite to the contrary, the attack was carried out as a war experiment whose objective was to develop a new system of terror bombing by destroying an entire town. As reporter George Steer described it, the attack took place in four phases:

1. A medium bombardment was carried out by six bombers and some fighters to alert the population and force them to enter the refuges, inside the perimeter of the village, which would become deadly traps due to the 250-kilos bombs with delayed fuses. This first wave of bombing would also attract emergency services to the urban center where the third wave of heavy bombardment would surprise them out in the open and at the mercy of the bombs. Finally, during this first bombing phase,

the experimental squadron of Rudolf von Moreau destroyed the water pipe system, so that the firemen would not have water with which to extinguish the fires produced by the incendiary bombs.

2. Later the fighters flew in circles over the village, generating a ring of fire and preventing anyone from escaping from the city center. The Heinkel He 51 ground attack aircraft could carry up to six ten-kilogram bombs.

3. The Junkers Ju 52 then executed a carpet bombardment, Koppelwurf (high density) type, from north to south, launching a mixture of destructive and incendiary bombs in the small area of the city center (the "corral") that reduced the village to rubble.

4. A second ring of fire of fighter and ground attack aircraft was generated in order to prevent the survivors from leaving the perimeter of fire, thus causing greater mortality.

15

The Market Day Bombing

Monday was market day in Gernika. As one of the many "perizaleak" or regular visitors to the weekly markets Uxua Madariaga remembered that

> We had greatly enjoyed our Mondays in Guernica. It was a market day but it was more than that. It was a fiesta day much like the days of August in Zarauz where I spent my childhood . . . Busloads of people came from cities all over Bizkaia to buy food and livestock, and for the entertainment. The trains were also full of people from the Bilbao area. People who owned grocery stores often bought most of their week's supply of fresh produce at the Guernica market. More people came to Guernica

after the war started because they could buy food from the farmers—food that was not rationed. We always tried to get our work done by noon on Monday. Then we shopped in the market where we would always see friends from Zarauz who were refugees like us. Later in the afternoon a big group of us would go for coffee or chocolate, The market would be over by then and the dance in the Plaza would start about six or seven o'clock—after the pelota games. The morning of the 26th was nice; I remember being happy about the day because I knew the clothes would dry when we hung them out. I just thought it was going to be another happy Monday.[1]

Alarm systems before the radar were very basic. As the only means of warning, the guards of Mount Kosnoaga waved flags when they saw planes approaching Gernika. Then, the guards in the tower of the Andra Mari church in town gave the alarm signal by slow bell strokes to announce alarm and rattle strokes to announce danger. Depending on their location in town, people needed about fifteen minutes on average to access one of the shelters.

But Gernika is only ten kilometers from

---

1.   Testimony of Uxua Makazaga. In Smallwood, *The Day Guernica Was Bombed*, 26.

the coast, so if the bombers approached from the north, entering Gernika from the sea, at an average speed of about two hundred kilometers an hour, the victims would not have but a maximum of three minutes to reach the shelters, so they would be caught by surprise, out in the open.

Italian fighter plane Fiat Cr.32.

However, despite this, the first attack was not made from the north. Quite the opposite. The first plane that bombed Gernika was a solitary ground attack aircraft Heinkel He 51 that before bombing made a series of turns west of the village. This plane was so seen, the guards rung the bells and civilians had plenty of time to time to reach the shelters. Many witnesses referred to that plane as the "snitch," the plane in charge of making sure that there was no anti-aircraft batteries in a certain place before the bombers attacked it. No one suspected that in reality its role was very different, because thanks to informants from Gernika the rebels knew that there were no anti-aircraft guns in town. The mission of that solitary Heinkel He 51 was to force the alarm signal and push the population into the shelters. Nobody could suspect that Franco had ordered the mobilization of 20 percent of all bombers and fighters available in the whole of the Iberian Peninsula to attack the crowded city center of Gernika with no protection other than some sixteen shelters, some of which were going to become deadly traps.

That day, Amaia Castillejo's bother and the ten-year-old altar boy Pablo Izagirre rang the bells of Andra Mari. Two soldiers, José R. Urtiaga and Antxon Zabalia were in Burgogana, an elevation of 190 meters over the Ajangiz neighborhood east of Gernika, when the first plane reached the town. It was 4:20 pm when they saw the first Heinkel He 51. "It was very low—lower than us—and was circling the town. We sat there smoking and watched it. Then, somewhere near the train station, it dropped some bombs. It also started machine gunning the people. That surprised us. The airplane continued in a big circle and disappeared from our view to the south. About three minutes later this same airplane, or one just like it, came back and again started circling the town, dropping bombs and machine gunning the people."[2]

---

2.   Testimony of Jose R. Urtiaga Makazaga. In Smallwood, *The Day Guernica Was Bombed*, 53.

That first attack caused the first deaths.

> I threw myself into a ditch full of water. Then several women came to me, their faces disarranged in terror; mad and hugging me, they stretched out in the same ditch. Their voices were dry, shrill screams. One of them was dressed in a black jacket and I tore off her jacket to better cover with it and with my tabard the remainder of her white dress and so prevent it from being seen by the aviators. Together we all cuddled, trembled, and prayed. When we were this way, I saw in the highway of Lekeitio a sad caravan of evacuees, oxen, cars, men and women who from the side of Kortezubi were coming to Gernika. The plane chased them; a bomb fell on them, the car was shattered, a cow jumped to pieces, and the woes of pain of men, women and children hurt our ears. Finally, at half past four, the plane left.[3]

The images were horrifying. As some of the witnesses remember, the bodies hit by the machine gun fire later appeared scattered around

3. Testimony of Iñaki Rezabal, La Roseraie, May 13 1938. José María Gamboa and Jean-Claude Larronde, eds., *La guerra civil en Euzkadi: 136 testimonios inéditos recogidos por José Miguel de Barandiarán* (Bidasoa: Milafranga, 2005), 637.

the village, broken into pieces by the intensity and power of the strafing.

Immediately after this first attack, two Heinkel He 111s and a Dornier Do 17 of the experimental bombing squadron led by Rudolf von Moreau coming from the Burgos air base flew over Gernika east-west. "We saw a formation of big airplanes coming from Mount Oiz," recalled Pedro Gezuraga, "we watched them fly past the town. Then they circled and flew right down the Bermeo Road. They were heading for the center of the town. Fear was in my father's eyes. In a feeble voice he said: 'Son, they're going to bomb Guernica. Leave the oxen. Go try to find your mother.' I left immediately. I was running down the road when I faintly heard my father warning me to be careful."[4] The planes dropped four tons of bombs on the city center and destroyed the water pumping system of the town. They were followed by one or two squadrons of Italian Savoia-Marchetti SM.79 bombers from Soria piloted by Captain Stefano Castellani, Lieutenant Porro, and Lieutenant Roberto Facaso, who dropped their cargo on the railway station and also on the city center. "A bomb fell and demolished several floors. The fragments of shrapnel and rubble fell around us, like rain . . . So we got up to take refuge near the railroad track . . . we ran, and the fighters machine-gunned us following our steps. They

---

4.   Testimony of Pedro Gezuraga. In Smallwood, *The Day Guernica Was Bombed*, 61.

shot all the people there. My mother fell ten meters away. We all ran through the railroad track while the planes were hovering over us . . . Five people from our group fell, killed . . . And I saw Gernika burning."[5]

Everyone believed that the bombing had ended but the people were instructed to stay in the shelters for a prudent amount of time until they were sure that no more planes were coming.

5.   Testimony of María Dolores Ribas, 18 years of age, taken by Paul Vaillant-Couturier. "Demain, Bilbao," *L'Humanité*, Thursday, May 13, 1937, 1-3.

16

Second Phase of the Bombing: The Circle of Fire

Only about twenty minutes to a half an hour had passed since the bombing began, when, immediately after this first wave of bombardment, the Italian Fiat Cr.32 and the German Messerschmitt Bf 109 fighter squadrons and the Heinkel He 51 ground attack aircraft (possibly supported by Breguet Br.19, Heinkel He 45, and Heinkel He 70) generated a ring of fire around Gernika. The purpose of these flights was to strafe anyone who tried to leave the urban area, which had begun to burn. Packed in the city center, and many of them locked in shelters, the fighters would keep them covered for the next half hour. In fact, although the attack against Gernika was a bombing, approximately half of the aircraft that participated in the attack were fighter planes.

The Heinkel He 51 ground attack aircraft had two MG 17 machine guns mounted on the engine each of which could fire twenty 7.92 x 57 millimeter bullets per second. In addition they loaded six ten-kilogram bombs. The Messerschmitt Bf 109 used bullets of an even larger caliber, 13 x 64 mm with a firing rate of fifteen rounds per second, capable of shooting down an aircraft. Flying in "chains" of three planes in line or "pattuglia in fila" formation, the first of the planes in the chain dove at speeds of around 250 kilometers per hour machine-gunning concentrations of people hidden under trees, supported by a parapet or inside a ditch. As noted by the soldier Joxe Iturria, whom the Luftwaffe fighters machine-gunned on numerous occasions since he was transporting trucks with ammunition, "the reaction of those who were not used to the war was to run away, and then they were lost."[1] At that moment, the second aircraft in the chain machine-gunned those who, in panic, had run away, descending well below a hundred meters and machine-gunning them (trench-attack method) and, finally, the "Kette" or the third plane of the chain descended machine-gunning and launching one or more of the ten-kilogram bombs.

As Iturria explained, "I survived because I laid on my back and stayed that way for the

---

1.   Interview with Joxe Iturria. Lesaka, May 17 and 21, June 7 and July 30, 2013. See also Joxe Iturria, *Memorias de Guerra* (Gernika: Gernika-Lumoko udala, 2013), 78.

three and a half hours the bombing lasted, without moving. Those pilots knew very well what they did, they machine-gunned everything that moved, and also those who laid face down."[2] As explained by a Luftwaffe fighter pilot: "You get hit all the same. We attacked from 10 metres, and when the idiots ran I had a good target. I had only just to hold my machine-gun. I am sure some of them got a full 22 bullets in them."[3]

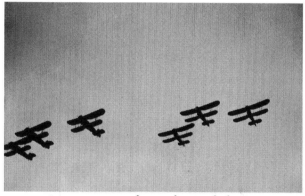

German ground attack Heinkel He51
planes in chain formation.

Imanol Agirre, a boy of just ten years old, lived it this way: "We saw terrible things. One man near us had been hunting. He ran across to take shelter in a hut and we saw the planes kill

---

2.   Ibid.

3.   Sönke Neitzel and Harald Welzer, eds., *Soldaten: On Fighting, Killing, and Dying. The Secret World War II Transcripts of German POWs* (Brunswick: Scribe Publications, 2012), 47.

both him and his dog. We saw a family of people we knew from our street run into a wood. There was the mother with two children and the old grandmother. The planes circled about the wood for a long time and at last frightened them out of it. They took shelter in a ditch. We saw the old granny cover up the little boy with her apron. The planes came low and killed them all in the ditch, except the little boy. He soon got up and began to wander across a field, crying. They got him too. It was terrible; we were both crying so much we could not speak. Everybody was being killed."[4]

Angeles Atxabal, a nurse at the Karmele Deuna hospital said that

> the bombs were crashing and window glass was flying everywhere. Yet we had to find places for the steady stream of wounded people that were coming into the hospital. All of our beds were full and we had to put the new arrivals on the floor. The few doctors that we had were trying to sort out the most serious cases. These were to be driven to hospitals in Bilbao at the first opportunity. Yet the bombing just went on and on, as did the flood of people

---

4.   Imanol Agirre wrote this letter at the Stoneham Camp (East Sussex) in July 1937. In Yvonne Cloud and Richard Ellis, *The Basque Children in England. An Account of Their Life at North Stoneham Camp* (London: Victor Gollancz Ltd., 1937), 56–57.

coming in to us. I was in despair because I was now seeing the torn bodies of my lifelong friends and neighbors. I didn't dare think of what might be happening to my family. Sometime during the first hour of the bombing, I heard the familiar voice of a woman calling my name. I turned and recognized the disheveled face of a woman who had been a neighbor of ours. She was holding the limp body of her little boy in her arms. I rushed to them, but instantly saw that the child was mortally wounded. Yet I found a place for them. The child went with the first people that were evacuated to Bilbao. He was probably dead when they left.[5]

María Olabarria, fifty-two years old, lost her two daughters:

Suddenly we heard the noise of the engines and we saw the flags raised. As we were in the outskirts, near the fields, we look for cover there, at full speed, my daughters and I and a neighbor. Immediately, from the place where we were we saw the bombs fall. The planes circled and circled above us. It seemed that they were looking for us.

---

5. Testimony of Angeles Atxabal. In Smallwood, *The Day Guernica Was Bombed*, 81.

And it was true: they were looking for four women. There was a house nearby. We ran toward the entrance. It was closed. Then we stuck materially to the door frame to protect each other. I was in the middle. An airplane circled the farmhouse, opening fire with the machine gun. Earth jumped in front of us. Suddenly we heard a frightful crunch: a bomb had fell on the farmhouse. The trepidation threw me to the ground among stones and bricks. My oldest daughter, who was twenty-seven, died instantly, crushed. The other, the youngest, who was going to get married, had time to hold my hand, squeeze it a little and exclaim: "Ouch!" She sighed, and with his eyes fixed on me, she died. I do not know how long I was there between my two dead daughters. The blood ran down my neck. After a while they picked me up.[6]

6.   Testimony of María Olabarria, transcribed by Paul Vaillant-Couturier. "La madre que vio morir a dos hijas," *La Voz*, Wednesday, May 26, 1937, 1-4.

17

Third Phase of the Bombing: The Junkers Ju 52s

Around 5:00 pm, coming from the north, from the sea, and therefore unnoticed, the three K/88 squadrons of Junkers Ju 52 bombers from the Burgos airport led by Lieutenant Karl von Knauer, Lieutenant Hans Henning von Beust, and Captain Erhart Krafft von Dellmensingen bombarded Gernika in seven groups of three aircraft each in two or more passes over an air corridor about 150 meters wide. This was the carpet bombing.

The Junkers launched an approximate total of thirty-one tons of explosive bombs of 250 kilograms and 50 kilograms with delayed fuses and thousands of incendiary bombs on the city center flying at a height of between six and eight hundred meters.[1] The Junkers carried the

---

1.   Effect of the bombings of Spanish cities (front of Bizkaia). May 28, 1937. *Heft 2, Führung, Abschnitte IV bis VI*, file RL 7/57b.

bombs in a special carrier or box called Elvemag ESAC-250. Each Ju 52 could load up to eight 250-kilogram bombs or 32 50-kilogram bombs (or other combinations of bombs of different weight and size) into the carriers, that is, something less than 2,000 kilograms of explosive.[2] But Richthofen knew that each Junkers could carry much more weight, up to a total of 3,080 kilograms,[3] so he ordered that boxes of incendiary bombs weighing 25 kilos each be loaded to be dropped by hand through the side gate of the bombers, which forced the pilots of the Junkers to make several passes over the village.[4]

The incendiary bombs were very small, weighing about a kilo, so when they were launched from the airplanes they did not acquire the necessary impulse to penetrate the buildings through the roofs. They simply burned the roof, and not the whole building. As a consequence, Richthofen ordered the 250-kilo bombs to be dropped first with two-second delay fuses. As it was experienced in the course of the

2.   Heinz J. Nowarra, *Junkers Ju 52, Aircraft & Legend* (Newbury Park, CA: Haynes, 1987), 36. See also Antony L. Kay and Paul Couper, *Junkers Aircraft and Engines, 1913–1945* (London: Putnam Aeronautical Books, 2004), 110.

3.   *L'Aviazione Tedesca al 10 gennaio 1936*. NARA, RG 242. *Foreign Records Seized Collection. Collection of Italian Military Records, 1935-1943*. Microfilm Publication T821, R. 214, 66-133.

4.   *Auswertung Rügen*. Heft 2, Führung, Abschnitte IV bis VI, legajo RL 7/57b. In Ángel Viñas, "Epílogo [a la nueva edición de la obra de Herbert Southworth, *La destrucción de Guernica*]" (Granada: Comares, 2013), 644.

bombing of Madrid, if the bombs exploded on contact with the roofs of the houses, the buildings would not fall apart. The 250 kilos bombs were able to completely tear down a five-story building but only if they exploded on the first floor, so they needed to be equipped with delay fuzes, because two seconds was the time needed to traverse the buildings as knives and explode on the ground floor, thus achieving the collapse of the whole building.

Priest blessing a Junkers Ju 52 before departure.

Once the buildings had been demolished and their wooden interior exposed, the incendiary bombs were dropped. Considering that most of the shelters were in the basements of these buildings, the people who had sought refuge there would die from the explosion and the subsequent demolition of the building or, if they survived this, they would die asphyxiated or burned under the ruins by the effect of the incendiaries, which raised the temperature initially to 2,500°C, consuming all the oxygen. The fires, at temperatures of 1,500°C, lasted for three days before they could be extinguished.

This phase of the bombing surprised the rescue services, firefighters, health personnel, and soldiers in the city center where they were trying to rescue survivors and quell the fires caused by the first wave of bombers. Juan Sistiaga was one of them:

> There was a big mansion just north of a small plaza in the northeast section of Guernica. The mansion had a stone wall around it and a bomb had fallen and broken part of the wall. Lying nearby were two girls and a man who must have taken refuge near the wall. The man and one of the girls were dead. The other girl was still alive, but her abdomen had been torn open and her intestines were hanging out. Her eyes were open and they seemed to be pleading to me for help. I knew that she was mortally wounded but I knelt down and she struggled to get up. I held her under the shoulders and tried to assure her that a stretcher was on the way and that we would take her to the hospital as soon as possible. She just looked at me. She never said

anything. She was a very beautiful girl with light brown hair. I was still holding her and talking to her, and waiting for a stretcher, when I heard the sound of airplanes. I looked back over my shoulder and saw them. They were those ugly three-motored German bombers. They were low and right upon us. I turned and looked back at the girl. She was dead.[5]

The shelters were crowded, people could barely breathe and "Bombs were dropping without a stop; we were almost choked with smoke and dust. But no bomb hit the factory. Factories are the safest places to be, far safer than hospitals."[6] Sebastián Uria, one of the few survivors of the shelter of Andra Mari remembered that

it didn't look like much of a refuge; it was just a street with a pine-reinforced roof over it but, for some reason, I went inside. As soon as I was inside, I knew that I had made a mistake. It was jammed with people. They were standing like sardines in a can. I wanted to get out of there. The bombers would be there any minute and

5. Testimony of Juan Sistiaga. In Smallwood, *The Day Guernica Was Bombed*, 66-67.

6. Imanol A. wrote this note at the Stoneham Camp (East Sussex) in July 1937. In Cloud and Ellis, *The Basque Children in England*, 56-57.

I didn't want to be trapped. I started working my way through the people and finally arrived at the other entry which opened onto another street. I debated to myself whether or not I should go outside and make a run for the mountain. I probably would have gone if I hadn't seen a vacant area just inside the refuge, near the entryway. There was only one other person there, an eighteen- or nineteen-year old girl who was crying. Apparently the others were afraid to be that close to the entryway. It seemed like a good place to me—at least there was enough light that I could see what was around me. But there wasn't much time now; I could hear the airplanes coming closer. I crouched down beside the girl and told her not to cry, that we would be all right. The noise of the airplanes kept getting louder and louder and then the girl blurted out to me that she had left her two baby brothers in the house above us and she had been afraid to go get them. That was why she was crying. But, I didn't have time to think about getting them. There was a loud roar of engines. The bombers were right on top of us . . . I was looking at the girl when I heard the whistle of bombs above us. Then there

was a tremendous blast. It knocked
me down. I fell over the girl and everything came down on top of us. I think
the girl was killed instantly . . . Then I
heard more explosions. They were getting closer. I prayed for another bomb
to fall right on top of me.[7]

A 250-kilo bomb falling at a speed of 450
km/h impacted directly against this shelter that
had no more protection than a roof of sandbags.
The bombs had a delay time of two seconds,
so they pierced the buildings like knives and
exploded at ground level, among the crowded
people in Andra Mari. Consequently, practically all of the 450 or 500 people who had sought
refuge there perished on the spot and others,
perhaps less fortunate, would die during the
night, as a consequence of the wounds, asphyxiated or burned by the fire and temperatures of
over 1,500°C. Some soldiers like Captain Joseba
Elosegi tried to rescue the victims, without
success, amid the horrible screams of pain that
came from inside the ruins. "I ran to a good
woman . . . who could not say but 'my son, my
son.' He dragged me to the pile of rubble that
had been his house. I started working like a
madman; removing stones and heavy wood-
en beams. I scratched my nails until I broke
them . . . When I touched the clothes of that

---

7.   Testimony of Sebastian Uria. In Smallwood, *The Day
      Guernica Was Bombed*, 69 and 73.

creature that was not more than three years old, I stained my hands with its blood, still warm. I took that broken and lifeless body and lifted it to his mother."[8]

Iñaki Rezabal also related what happened:

> Laid against the ground, I raised my head a little, I looked up with eyes of horror, I saw an aircraft, on his wings I read Junker, and I saw two men in its cabin. I noticed that something was tearing the air at the speed of lightning. Then, a terrible noise; It was a light bomb that exploded over my body. I trembled, I was electrified, my breathing stopped, I cried out in pain and I was buried in earth, stones and smoke. Fighting desperately, I got up. A great sorrow stirred me. My left arm was broken. Ten centimeters below the joint of the shoulder, I had a deep wound from which blood gushed out and, falling through my body, burned me. With my broken flesh and the arm bone fractured, my left forearm, hanging from tendons, was mixed with earth. I crouched down and, with a serenity that I never thought I would have, I first grabbed my injured arm with my right hand and, horrified,

---

8.   Joseba Elosegi, *Quiero morir por algo* (Barcelona: Plaza y Janés, 1977), 130.

instinctively crossed it on my back. I felt the blood coming down from the shoulder to the feet like a river of fire through my clothes. As crazy I started walking without a fixed orientation. I screamed and asked for help. The planes were still bombing. I was crossing corpses of women and children who had been killed by the bombs and machine guns of the planes as they were trying to flee. Ayes of dying and near dead shattered my ears. I would never forget that tragic picture in which a woman held a little child in her arms and to her chest. The boy shouted: "Amatxo, hiltzera noa" ["mother, I am going to die"], and the mother wrapping her little son with her disheveled hair, while running unconsciously, at random, answered: "Ez beldurtu ume; biak hilko gara" ["do not be afraid son, we will die together"]. The mother had barely finished speaking when an airplane, diving to twenty meters, machine-gunned them and killed them both.[9]

---

9.   Iñaki Rezabal, La Roseraie, 13 de mayo de 1938. Gamboa and Larronde, eds., *La guerra civil en Euzkadi*, 637-38.

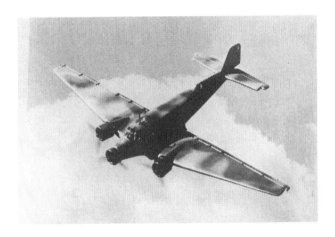

German bomber Junkers Ju 52.

*Fires caused by the first waves of
bombers over Gernika.*

18

Fourth Phase of the Bombing: Aerial Machine Gunning

The bombing had lasted one hundred at this point. For the next one hundred minutes, the Heinkel He 51s and Messerschmitt Bf 109s, supported by Fiat Cr.32s, generated a circle of fire around Gernika for the second time, machine-gunning and bombing the survivors who were now desperately trying to escape from the flames in town. This was how Juliana Itza recalled it:

> I was lying in the ditch, trembling with fear. An airplane was coming right over the top of us, firing its machine guns at everything. Then a bomb fell. It was a terrible explosion. It hit just behind me. I wasn't hurt, but I was afraid to look back. A man had taken refuge in a hole that was just behind me. The

bomb must have fallen on him. Finally I raised up. It was horrible. There were pieces of him everywhere. On the other side of me there was a woman who had been covering her grandson with her body. She had been killed by the bullets. The boy was unhurt. Another woman rushed to the boy and covered him with her own body. The machine guns had also killed a young man and his girlfriend who were refugees from Guipuzkoa. I couldn't believe it. I just couldn't believe it. It was like living in a nightmare. "Go away, go away, please go away," I kept praying. But it was not to be. The airplanes just kept coming and coming with their bombs and machine guns. I think they were trying to kill every single person in Guernica.[1]

And so it was. As noted by Robert Mackinnon, head of the aeronautical research department of the British navy, Hans J. Wandel, who piloted a Heinkel He 51 on Gernika that April 26, testified that they had been ordered "to strafe from the air anything moving."[2]

---

1.   Testimony of Juliana Itza. In Smallwood, *The Day Guernica Was Bombed*, 84.

2.   "Los aviones que bombardearon Guernica y que actúan en el frente vasco son alemanes, conducidos por pilotos de la misma nacionalidad," *Ahora*, Sunday, May 30, 1937, p. 8. See also, "Un informe sensacional de Mr. Mackinnon,

Gernika in flames after the bombing.

Civilians did not know how to react to aircraft attacks. Such is the case of Kattalin, a young woman, married and with two children, who, scared by the planes, ran down the road south of Gernika. She had a roll of wire in her arms when a plane flew low above the house and fired its machine guns at her. Mikel Barazpe's wife shouted at her to go home before they killed her and bombed their house. Kattalin,

jefe del departamento de investigaciones aeronáuticas de la marina inglesa, sobre el bombardeo de Gernika," *El Sol*, Sunday, May 30, 1937, first page. Hemeroteca Municipal de Madrid (HMM).

Gernika in flames the night after the bombing.

still at the door, was sweaty and excited and exclaimed, "these planes have tried to kill me!" She just could not believe that someone wanted to kill her. But she was too afraid to sit still inside that house, and ran outside again. As Mikel Barazpe said, that "we tried to discourage this idea, but it was of no use. She left and we wished her well. Then, about ten minutes later, the airplanes came back again. They were diving and shooting at everything that moved. One airplane caught us by surprise while we were out in the entryway. It came right down over the rooftop with its machine guns firing. After it left, leaves from our trees were still drifting to the ground. We later learned that Kattalin went to the bakery, left her roll of wire, and asked them to deliver it with her bread the next day. Then she went back out on the road and had just gotten to the junction of the cemetery road when an airplane came down firing its machine guns. Later someone else found her lying at the base of the cemetery road, just under the embankment. She was dead. Her body was riddled with bullets. One had entered the back of her head and passed out just above her eye."[3]

The last plane left Gernika around 7:40 pm.

---

3.   Testimony of Mikel Barazpe. In Smallwood, *The Day Guernica Was Bombed*, p. 47.

19

Result

Between thirty-one and forty-six tons of bombs were dropped on Gernika. The city center was totally razed. Of all of buildings in town, 85.22 percent—a total of 271—were completely destroyed and 99 percent of the buildings were affected. Only 1 percent of the constructions were saved from the effects of the bombing. The incendiary bombs caused a fire that could not be extinguished until April 29. In line with the concept of terror bombing, the armament factories, the railway line, and the Errenteria bridge, the only strategic objectives in town, were not bombed.

As Castor Uriarte said, "the truth is I don't know of anything of a significant military nature that was destroyed in that bombing."[1] But

---

1. Testimony of Castor Uriarte. In Smallwood, *The Day Guernica Was Bombed*, p. 108.

it was a war experiment and after the bombing the town was closed to study the effects of the attack by order of General Emilio Mola.[2] After examining the ruins and despite having thrown about forty tons of bombs without having even touched the bridge of Errenteria that allegedly was the target of the bombing, Richthofen recorded in his diary that the bombing had been a "complete technical success,"[3] since Gernika was destroyed in a record time with a minimum cost, without any losses and, it was possible to keep the population immobile, within the perimeter of the town, during the entire duration of the attack.

It was also a surgical bombardment that affected exclusively the urban area of the town that was what was intended to destroy (the inner marked area). Just ten meters from the railroad track to the city center everything was destroyed, while ten meters out of this same road, the industrial sector did not suffer any impact. San Juan and Portu streets, which were no more than fifteen meters wide, also separated the totally destroyed area (from these streets to the interior of Gernika) from the zone that hardly suffered any damage (toward the exterior of the village). Finally, the Asilo Calzada

---

2.   Al general jefe de Flechas Negras en Deba. Instrucciones sobre operaciones, Vitoria-Gasteiz, 28 de abril de 1937. USSME, f. 18.

3.   Maier, Klaus A., *Guernica. La intervención alemana en España y el "caso Guernica,"* Sedmay, Madrid, 1976, p. 128.

*Gernika surgically destroyed: the city
center after the bombing.*

street, even narrower than the previous ones,
divided precisely the part affected by the bombs
from what was not touched. It can be observed
how the trees of the western part of the Pasileku
preserved their leaves intact after the bombing while those located to the east are totally
burned.

Desolation was absolute. Mathieu Corman,
correspondent of *Ce Soir*, wrote: "No, Dante did
not see anything . . . We are in a place where we
cannot breathe. No more leaves in the trees; the
bare trunks are twisted in the dark, reddened,
death. The walls that are still standing present
in their facades the scars of the bombs and the
shrapnel. And those little abrasions: airplane
bullets . . . Here and there, a vague shape in a
red night, a corpse, man or beast. The smoke

sometimes brings a smell of burned flesh. Nightmare. The corpses show extravagant injuries. Here, an open head like a coconut, with the brain out. There, an arm, a leg torn off; a naked bone of flesh. There, too, a sectioned body, as if a sadistic murderer had sunk his knife into his belly and side, with all his fury. Some corpses showed only traces of bullets. I will never forget, I will never forget, that girl, still beautiful in death, half naked because of an explosion, whose belly was just a mass of blood. She maintained a vivid expression, as if her sudden and intense joy of living had been surprised by dying so young."[4]

Just after the bombing the work of recovering and recording the dead and wounded started but the next morning the cries of the victims buried alive under the rubble could still be heard. Sabin Apraiz, a member of the General Staff of the Basque Army remembered it this way: "I went to the Santa Maria Refuge and it was completely covered with rubble. Fires were burning close to it, but people were desperately trying to free the people who were trapped. I joined those who were working, but it was hopeless. We could hear the people down in the rubble calling to us and moaning and we worked as hard as we could. But there was too much rubble covering them and the fires were increasing in size and getting closer all the time.

---

4.   Mathieu Corman, ¡*Salud camarada! Cinq mois sur les fronts d'Espagne*, Editions Tribord, Paris, 1937, pp. 293-295.

Finally, we had to abandon them. By this time I was almost like a crazy man."[5]

Captain Joseba Elosegi, the highest-ranking soldier that day in Gernika, recounted how the cries of those people still alive under the rubble could be heard but, despite the fact that they worked by piecework, they could never rescue them. They died a slow death, in absolute darkness, burned by the advance of the flames over the rubble under which they were trapped. And everything was surrounded by "a tragic

Ruins of Gernika.

5. Testimony of Sabin Apraiz. In Smallwood, *The Day Guernica Was Bombed*, p. 112.

Ruins of Gernika.

color and an air that smells of burned flesh."[6] As Augusto Barandiaran, one of the doctors at Karmele Deuna's hospital, assured, "The next morning I left the hospital and went with some men to look at the refuges where people were buried. There were reports that some of the people were still alive. I saw the long refuge that had been built in one of the streets. I don't know how anybody could be alive in that one. I looked at both ends; both were covered with tons of material. I stayed in the town another two days, working in the hospital. I know they hadn't gotten any people out of the refuges by then. Mola's troops came in after that and I don't think they were in any hurry to dig out

6.   Joseba Elosegi, *Quiero morir por algo*, Plaza y Janés, Barcelona, 1977, p. 137.

those people. Considering this time factor, and
the fact that these refuges were in the center of
the town where the fire was the most intense,
I can't believe that any of the people who died
there were ever identified."[7]

Francisca Arriaga declared the same: "I went
back into the town the next morning. It was
gray and cloudy. Some of the fires were burning
and some were smoking. I went down Calle San
Juan and under the Renteria Bridge I saw the
body of Felipe Basterretxea. He was lying face
up near a small boat. I crossed the bridge and
continued down Calle San Juan. When I got near
the refuges, I could hear human sounds coming
from them. There were some people still alive
under all that debris. There were mountains of
material over some of them. It would have been
impossible to dig them out. I would rather die
than see such horror again."[8]

Ángeles Atxabal, a nurse at the same hospital, said that "the hospital was chaotic. My
nerves were at the breaking point. And, now
that the bombing was over, I couldn't get my
family out of my mind. Finally, something in
me snapped. Some impulse drove me out of the
hospital and through the rubble in search of my
family. The reality of the fire and destruction
soon brought me back to my senses. I tried to

7.   Testimony of Augusto Barandiaran. In Smallwood, *The Day Guernica Was Bombed*, 124-25.

8.   Testimony of Francisca Arriaga. In Smallwood, *The Day Guernica Was Bombed*, 124.

go down Calle San Juan, but that was impossible. The San Juan Church was in flames and the tower would fall at any moment. I turned and picked my way along Calle Chorroburu but I found no one who knew of my family. Finally, I went back to the hospital. I had a sick feeling inside—a feeling that my family was dead. I spent the entire night at the hospital. We did our best, but that amounted to little more than finding room on the floor for the arrivals. Trucks and ambulances were taking the most seriously wounded to Bilbao hospitals via the Bermeo Road. But, for most of the night our floors were covered with people and blood."[9]

During three days the recovery of identifiable bodies and pieces of bodies that, collected with baskets, would be incinerated in the Ibarra square of San Juan was carried out in order to avoid the spread of diseases. Three days after having been recovering and searching bodies, on April 29 there were still corpses in the streets.

---

9.   Testimony of Angeles Atxabal. In Smallwood, *The Day Guernica Was Bombed*, 105.

20

Death Toll

As a result of this enormous display of strength, the number of deaths was large.

Each and every one of the thirty-nine witnesses—among them the seven international reporters who were in Gernika the day of the bombing—who at the time of the events revealed a death toll estimated that more than eight hundred people had lost their lives in the bombing. For example, the British journalist George Steer, a correspondent for *The Times*, calculated that at least eight hundred people perished in Gernika.[1] Noel Monks, Australian

---

1. Steer, George, "The Tragedy of Guernica. Town Destroyed in Air Attack," *The Times*, Wednesday, April 28, 1937, 17; "Historic Basque Town Wiped Out; Rebel Fliers Machine-Gun Civilians," *New York Times*, Wednesday, April 28, 1937, 1. See also George Steer, "Basque Town Wiped Out by Rebel Planes," *Manchester Guardian*, Wednesday, April 28, 1937 (press Association Foreign Special in Bil-

correspondent of the *Daily Express*, was the first
reporter to arrive at the site after the bombing.
As reported to Paris *Soir* and the *Daily Express*
on April 27, Monks saw six hundred bodies
exposed to be recognized by their relatives or
friends before being buried. Monks said the
death toll was more than a thousand and added
that many bodies had been burned or mutilated so it would be very difficult to make an ex-
haustive record of the victims.[2] British Consul

---

bao, April 27; Steer wrote in first person, "Today I visited
what remains of the town"); "Destruction of Guernica.
Insurgent Denials," *The Times*, Thursday, April 29, 1937,
16; "El caso de Guernica" [that combines Monks' and
Steer's declarations], *Avance*, Friday, May 7, 1937, 2. And
"Die 'Times' bombardiert Guernica," *Nachmittags-Aus-
gabe. Deutsches Nachrichtenbüro*, Berlín, May 3, 1937, 1.
PAAA, R. 29753. In the British Library (BL).

2.   Monks, Noel, "I Saw the German Planes Bomb Guernica,"
Daily Express, Tuesday, May 1, 1937, p. 10. This article was
reproduced in various newspapers: "Je jure que ce sont les
avions allemands de Franco qui ont bombardé Guernika,"
Journal des Nations, Saturday, May 15, 1937; "El 'Yo Acu-
so' de un periodista inglés. Puedo jurar que los aviadores
alemanes de Franco bombardearon Guernica: yo digo al
mundo lo que vi," *Tierra Vasca*, Tuesday, May 18, 1937, 1;
"Puedo jurar que los aviadores alemanes de Franco bombardearon Guernica. Yo digo al mundo lo que vi," *La Tar-
de*, Tuesday, May 18, 1937, 3; "La emoción producida en
el mundo entero por la destrucción de Guernika," *Euzko
Deya*, Thursday, May 27, 1937, 5. Apart from the mentioned article, other articles of Monks were reproduced in
a large number of newspapers: "First Pictures of Bombed
Basque City. Taken by *Daily Express* Staff Reporter. Here
an Eyewitness Tells his Story. Gernika after the Air Horror, Special *Daily Express* Picture," *Daily Express*, Thursday, April 29, 1937, pp. 1-2 & 24. "Guernica détruite de
fond en comble par les avions," *Paris Soir*, Thursday, April

Ralph C. Stevenson, who visited the ruins of Gernika while preparing his report for British Ambassador Sir Henry Chilton, said that according to preliminary information available, the exact number of deaths would never be known, but he estimated that there would be at least three thousand casualties.[3]

However, more people were going to die as a result of their injures in the following weeks. After making a record of the people who lost their lives after the events in different Basque hospitals, the Basque Government registered 1,654 deaths between April and June 1937. But the Basque authorities expressed that the victims had been more since, apart from the people who lost their lives in hospitals or who were registered between April 26 and 29 in Gernika, the bodies of those who were buried under the debris were never rescued nor, therefore, registered.[4]

29, 1937, last page. "J'ai assité au bombardement de Guernica par les avions allemands," *Paris Soir*, Friday, April 30, 1937, last page. "El caso de Guernica," *Avance*, Friday, May 7, 1937, 2.

3. Report of Ralph C. Stevenson, British Consul in Bilbao, to Sir Henry Chilton. Bilbao, April 28, 1937. In, W. N. Medlicott and Dakin Douglas, eds., *Documents on British Foreign Policy (1919-1939), Second Series, Volume XVIII, European Affairs (January 2-June 30, 1937)* (London: Her Majesty's Stationery Office, 1980), 696-698.

4. *Relación de víctimas causadas por la aviación facciosa en sus incursiones del mes de abril de 1937*, IRARGI, Euskadiko Dokumentu Ondarearen Zentroa = Centro de Patrimonio Documental de Euskadi, Doc. GE-0037-03.

*Burning debris the morning after the
attack.*

As stated by Jose Labauria, Joxe Iturria,
and Maria Medinabeitia, between 450 and 500
people perished in the shelter of Andra Mari
and their corpses were never recovered or registered by the Francoist authorities after cap-
turing Gernika.[5] All three witnesses were on
this refuge trying to rescue still living people,
but they could not do anything. The fire finally
devoured those who were trapped alive inside
the ruins. As Labauria expressed, "those who
were in the refuge located between Artekale
and Barrenkale (there were about 450 people
in it) were all killed, as a result of a bomb that
fell on the Ribera butchery and knocked down
the building on whose side the shelter was

5.   Testimony of María Medinabeitia, Baiona, August 30,
      1937. In Gamboa and Larronde, eds., *La guerra civil en
      Euzkadi*, 173.

attached, collapsing this envelope the refugees there."[6] Joxe Iturria, who stood on the said refuge, also affirmed that all the survivors of the shelter were buried under the ruins. "I was in that shelter. The screams could be heard coming from under the ruins. They died all scorched and we could not do anything. There were 500 people there."[7]

Their bodies were never recovered or registered. On the contrary, the coup authorities tried to erase any evidence of the bombing. The cleaning up of the rubble in Gernika did not start until February 1939 and by the end of 1941 the prisoners of war forced to carry out this task had not finished their work. After collecting more than sixty thousand cubic meters of rubble during three years of work, the authorities reported no deaths.[8] As stated by the mayor of Gernika, "Our people, who had died and who were buried under the debris of our town, lost the right to be remembered."[9] The records of the deceased in Gernika and the adjacent towns

6. Jose Labauria, La Roseraie, April 2, 1938. In Gamboa and Larronde, eds., *La guerra civil en Euzkadi*, 604.

7. Interview with Joxe Iturria. Lesaka, May 17 and 21, June 7 and July 30, 2013. See also Iturria, *Memorias de Guerra*, 78.

8. Ministerio de Gobernación. Dirección General de Regiones Devastadas. Comisión de Vizcaya, *Desescombro de Guernica*, Bilbao, diciembre 24, 1941, p. 1. GBDZ, Regiones devastadas, Caja 3, Carp. 1. See also, Ángel B. Puente, *Reconstrucción de Guernica, Munguía, Maruri, Gatica, Bilbao*, 1941, 19. FSS, ATV 6453.

9. Smallwood, *The Day Guernica Was Bombed*, 9.

were erased, pages of some of these registers were removed and attempts were made to erase the names of the dead from the books of the deceased of the adjacent parishes.[10]

After the rebel forces led by General Emilio Mola took the village three days after the bombing, no effort was made to establish an exact number of deaths. Moreover, Franco ordered a report to counteract the damage that the propagation of news on the bombing of Gernika in neutral countries such as the United Kingdom or the United States was causing. The authors of the resulting Herrán Report, published exclusively in English for distribution in the United Kingdom, concluded that Gernika had been destroyed by the retreating "reds" and that virtually no people were in town when a "small bombing" began. The authors of the report finally declared that the dead in the "fire" of Gernika were less than a hundred: "The loss of life on April 26 was less than 100 persons. The evidence for this is partly negative, but is in general adequate to support this conclusion, and no evidence putting the casualties substantially higher has been brought forward even by Mr. Steer. Assuming this figure to be approximately correct it strongly suggests that aerial

10.   Humberto Unzueta, "Gernikako bonbaketa: Hildakoak. 1937-4-26," Gernika, 1992, 21-22. Also Humberto Unzueta, "Los muertos inoportunos," *Aldaba Gernika-Lumoko Aldizkaria*, No. 86, March–April, 1997, 42. See also, *Sustrai Erreak 2, Guernica 1937*, Aldaba-Gernikazarra, Gernika-Lumo, 2012, 331.

bombardment cannot have played a large part
... The conclusions to be drawn from the facts
summarized under these headings are clear and
unmistakable. By far the greater part of the destruction worked in Guernica was the deliber-
ate work of the retreating forces, and that part,
if any, which was the result of the air raid of the
26th could have been localized and, in so far as
the fires were concerned, substantially mitigat-
ed by prompt action on the early evening of the
26th ... The lesson which it teaches is no parti-
san doctrine. It is a strikingly frank document
and bears on it the impress of truth."[11]

Among the authors who have studied the
bombing of Gernika in depth, professors Paul
Preston,[12] Herbert R. Southworth,[13] William
Smallwood,[14] Angel Viñas,[15] and Xabier Irujo[16]
have found no evidence that the death toll
registered by the Basque Government was

---

11. *Guernica. Being the Official Report of a Commission Appointed by the National Government to Investigate the Causes of
the Destruction of Guernica on April 26-28, 1937*, Eyre &
Spottiswoode Ltd., London, 1938, p. IV. See also, Irujo,
Xabier, *Gernika: 26 de abril de 1937*, Crítica, Barcelona, pp.
209-213.

12. Preston, Paul, *La muerte de Guernica* (Barcelona: Debate,
2017).

13. Herbert R. Southworth, *Guernica! Guernica!: A Study of
Journalism, Diplomacy, Propaganda, and history* (Berkeley:
University of California Press, 1977), 353-370.

14. Smallwood, *The Day Guernica Was Bombed*, 9-10.

15. Ángel Viñas, "Prólogo," in Xabier Irujo, *Gernika: 26 de
abril de 1937* Barcelona: Crítica, 2018), 7-11.

16. Irujo, *Gernika 1937*, 101-19.

Lieutenant Joseba Elosegi on top of the ruins the morning after the attack. As Elosegi told me, when this photograph was taken he was listening to the cries of the people alive asking for their lives from under the rubble.

exaggerated or false. There is no evidence to indicate that any of the thirty-nine eyewitnesses who recorded more than a thousand deaths were lying. Southworth and Irujo assume that the death toll must be greater than the official number.[17] We have to add at least the 450 to 500 people who died in the Andra Mari shelter to the death toll registered by the Basque Government, and that gives us a death toll of at least two thousand people.[18]

---

17.   Southworth, *Guernica! Guernica!*, 353-370. Irujo, *Gernika 1937*, 101-19.

18.   Irujo, *Gernika*, 181-202.

Ruins of the Andra Mari shelter where from 450 to 500 people lost their lives.

Faced with this historiographical current, other authors have preferred to consider the death toll registered in the Herrán Report as correct, stating that a death toll of more than three hundred is exaggerated. Joachim von Ribbentrop, ambassador of Nazi Germany in Great Britain, was the first person to point out that a greater number of people had lost their lives elsewhere, suggesting that the number of deaths in Gernika had been minimal, thus attenuating the circumstances of what happened on April 26.[19] Adolph Galland, a member of the staff of the Condor Legion and author of *The First and the Last*, referred to the bombardment of

---

19. Telegram of Sir George Ogilvie-Forbes, attaché of the British embassy in Berlin, to Anthony Eden, April 29, 1937. In Medlicott and Douglas, eds., *Documents on British Foreign Policy*, 688.

Ruins of the Andra Mari shelter.

the city as a small side effect of the attack on the
Errenteria Bridge.[20] Other authors have tried
to reduce the magnitude of the bombing, the
intensity of the attack or the number of people
killed in Gernika. Ricardo de la Cierva, director
of popular culture and president of the national institute of Spanish books under the Franco
dictatorship, declared in 1970 that "not even a
dozen" people died in Gernika;[21] General Jesús

20.   Adolf Galland, *The First and the Last: The German Fighter
       Force in World War II* (London: Methuen, 1955), 26. See
       also Adolf Galland, *Die Ersten und die Letzten: die Jagd-
       flieger im zweiten Weltkrieg* (Darmstadt: F. Schneekluth,
       1953).

21.   "El mito de Guernica, donde no murieron ni siquiera una
       docena," interview by Pascual, Pedro, "La Guerra del 36,
       su historia y su circunstancia," *Arriba*, Madrid, Saturday,
       January 31, 1970. See also Southworth, *Guernica, Guerni-
       ca*, 363. In "La polémica y la verdad sobre Guernica," De
       la Cierva stated "the death toll was high—about one hun-
       dred—but it did not reach the fantastic figures of the pro-
       paganda that counted the deaths by thousands," *España*

Salas, whose brother was a pilot of the Francoist air force during the war, declared that some 120 people lost their lives in the bombing.[22]

1930-1936: La historia se confiesa, No. 45 December 1976, 297. See also De la Cierva "Guernica: los documentos contra el mito," *Nueva y definitiva historia de la guerra civil* (Madrid: DINPE, 1986).

22. Jesús Salas, *Guernica* (Madrid: Rialp, 1987), 36-37, 163-167, and 308-312.

21

"A Complete Technical Success"

The attack turned out to be a novel combination of Koppelwurf bombing (high density bombardment by increasing the number of explosive and incendiary bombs launched within a close area) and shuttle bombing or chain bombing, subsequent waves of aircraft acting over the time on the same target. In the event that the town had been a military objective, and the civilians had been troops defending it, by means of uninterrupted bombing and machine-gunning it would have been possible to keep them neutralized within the circle of fire, which would have allowed the infantry to advance and take the ruins without resistance by assault.

It was an empirical demonstration that the victory in "the next war" depended on the air force and Warsaw, Frampol, and Stalingrad were bombed following a very similar scheme by units under Richthofen's command. The bombing was in Richthofen's words "a complete technical success,"[1] the empirical demonstration that Göring was in possession of Thor's hammer, terror bombing or the most powerful weapon of the Third Reich. Like Kabul in 1919, Gernika had shown that a war could be won from the air, and that "the next war" would end with a crushing bombardment of terror. And indeed that's how it happened.

On May 13, 1937, Heinkel He 51 pilot Hans J. Wandel, the Gnome, was shot down and captured near Larrabetzu. As he testified, when he was shot down, he was experiencing the effectiveness of aerial machine-gunning at elevations of nine hundred, six hundred, and five hundred meters by counting the targets he obtained, naturally mostly civilians. The soldier who seized him removed his wallet from him and found a postcard for his girlfriend Else. It read: "Spain is a great country. We can destroy it in a few weeks. Yesterday we buried a village [Gernika]."[2]

---

1.   Maier, *Guernica*, 124.

2.   "El prisionero de ayer: Wandel hace la experiencia de los 500 metros," *El Liberal* 37, No. 12.598, May 14, 1937, 1 and 3.

22

"Tomorrow Bilbao . . ."

A terror bombing consists of an indiscriminate attack against a defenseless urban center with the intention of undermining the morale of the enemy and thus forcing its surrender. Following this logic, the Spanish, German, and Italian commands, in addition to Cardinal Gomá, maximum hierarch of the Spanish Catholic Church, informed the Basque government by various means that if the surrender of the Basque troops was not immediate, Bilbao would suffer the same fate as Gernika.

Franco threatened to excommunicate all Basques who had opposed his coup and assured that "we will be carriers of the destruction that war begets."[1] As the US ambassador Claude Bowers expressed and the local press recorded,

---

1.   Leaflet. In the Archive of the Foreign Ministry in Rome, USSME, f. 18.

Hans J. Wandel.

the day after the bombing General Mola threatened for the second time to raze Bizkaia: "We will destroy Bilbao, and its site, naked and desolate, will take away the desire of the British to assist against our will the Basque Bolsheviks."[2] Cardinal Isidro Gomá advised the Basque canon Alberto Onaindia to recommend to the Basque authorities the immediate surrender of Basque troops as the only means to prevent the destruction of Bilbao, because "whichever side is responsible for the destruction of Guernica, it is a terrible warning for the great city."[3]

2.   "Le général Mola annonce la destruction de Bilbao," *Ce Soir*, jueves, 29 de abril de 1937, p. 23. See also the report of Claude G. Bowers to Cordell Hull, Secretary of State. Donibane Lohitzune, May 5, 1937. NARA, U.S. Department of State Files 1930-1939 (Files 852.00/..., Boxes 6386 to 6407), Document 852.00/5427.

3.   Letter of Cardinal Isidro Gomá to Alberto Onaindía, May 5, 1937. Reproduced by Paul Preston in *The Destruction of*

Ruins of Gernika.

But the Basque Government did not surrender and, consequently, the aerial bombardments on civilian populations were outstandingly accentuated. As pointed out by the military attaché of the US embassy, Colonel Stephen O. Fuqua, in a report on the military

Guernica (London: HarperCollins Publishers Ltd., 2017), quote from ebook version. In *The Spanish Holocaust: Inquisition and Extermination in Twentieth-Century Spain* (London: HarperCollins Publishers Ltd., 2008), Preston also reproduces and discusses this letter. See also, José Andrés Gallego and Antonio M. Pazos, eds., *Documentos de la guerra civil. 5: Abril–Mayo de 1937* (Madrid: CESIC, 2003), 357.

situation dated April 28, 1937, the bombings intensified on the Basque front in order to break the morale of the Basque militias."[4]

The scale of the raids became dreadful. Prior to the bombing of Gernika, more than six hundred bombing operations had taken place on Basque soil. But the number of bombing operations increased drastically from April 20. In April 1937, 250 bombing operations were carried out, and in May the number of operations was increased to 300, with an average of about ten operations per day. Goring ordered bombing with special intensity on May 12 because that day of the coronation of King George VI of England was celebrated in London.[5] In the first two weeks of May, one of the hardest phases of the war, 158 bombing operations took place: fifteen consecutive days of uninterrupted bombing and an average of 10.53 operations per day. In the whole of the war in the Basque Country, from July 22, 1936 to August 18, 1937 (397 days of war), more than a thousand bombing operations were carried out, with an average of 2.7 operations per day for the year.[6]

4. Report of Stephen O. Fuqua, military attaché of the American embassy in Donibane Lohitzune, to Cordell Hull, Secretary of State. Donibane Lohitzune, April 28, 1937. NARA, U.S. Department of State Files 1930-1939 (Files 852.00/..., Boxes 6386 to 6407), Document 852.00/5325.

5. "Hitler is celebrating Coronation Day with the biggest air-raid and bombardment on this city [Bilbao] since the offensive began," *The Daily Worker*, London, May 12, 1937.

6. Xabier Irujo, "Bombardeos en Euskadi (1936-1937)," in

Ruins of Gernika.

The amount of explosive dropped was also tremendous. The Italian air command dropped 40,545 bombs on the Basque Country between the beginning of April and the middle of June 1937, an absolute total of 446,450 kilos of explosive in 106 days of war or an average of 4.2 tons per day. The flight journal of the Aviazione Legionaria for the month of May

Joseba Agirreazkuenaga and Mikel Urkijo, eds., *Senderos de la memoria: Relación de espacios vinculados a la memoria de la guerra civil y el exilio.* (Leioa: Grupo de investigación Biography & Parliament de la Universidad del País Vasco, 2016), vol. 2, 177–228.

of 1937 establishes that 722 tons of bombs had been thrown in the Basque front.[7] The Condor Legion dropped an even greater number of incendiary and explosive bombs and there are no records of the amount of explosive launched by Spanish air units, all of which gives us a frightening minimum balance. According to the information provided by Rear Admiral Boehm, in the last six weeks before the fall of Bilbao German planes dropped eight hundred tons of bombs.[8] This means an average of 133 tons per week or 19 tons a day until the fall of Bilbao. All this gives us a minimum of 1.2 million kilograms of bombs dropped on Bizkaia in two and a half months, and an average of more than 25 tons per day until the fall of Bilbao. And to this it is necessary to add the amount of explosive dropped by the Spanish air units.

7.   *Aviazione*, AMAE, Gabinetto del Ministro, Busta 1236, 1-10.

8.   War Diary of the commander of the observation forces, Rear Admiral Boehm. Entry of May 13, 1937. In Maier, *Guernica*, 145.

23

The Bombing in International Headlines

The first international reporters to report on the bombing were Noel Monks, George Steer, Christopher Holme, Mathieu Corman, and Scott Watson. Monks was the first international reporter to arrive in Gernika and the only one who saw the bombing from the outskirts. Corman, Steer, and Monks would each dedicate a chapter to the bombing in their respective memoirs.

The news quickly spread throughout the world to become front-page news in most of the newspapers of the European and American democracies and thousands of articles covered the news. In the United States alone more than seven thousand articles are recorded about the bombing between the end of April and the beginning of July 1937. Of article published by the *New York Times*, forty of the sixty-three articles

(63 percent) between April 27 and July 4, 1937 refer to the total destruction of the village and, 80 percent of the articles published on April 27 in American newspapers about the bombing were published on the front page.[1]

Noel Monk's article in the Daily News.

Bomb holes in Gernika as the ones described by the international reporters.

1.   Irujo, *Gernika 1937*, 129-30.

24

Franco Orders a Cover-Up

On April 27, Franco ordered the denial of statements made by the Basque president Jose A. Agirre in relation to the rebel bombardments, and also ordered that "the fierce system of the Reds to set afire all the cities before the withdrawal" be denounced.[1] Accordingly, the press and the radio controlled and censored by the dictatorships involved in the bombing denied that Gernika had been bombed and claimed that the town had been burned by the Basques themselves in retreat. Franco ordered the writing of two reports that concluded that Gernika had been set afire by the Basques: the Machimbarrena-Milán del Bosch report (published in Vitoria-Gasteiz on May 1, 1937)

---

1. *Operazioni di Bilbao*. Telegram of General Carlo Bossi. Salamanca, April 27, 1937. AMAE, Gabinetto del Ministro (1923-1943), Busta 7 (Uffizio Spagna Leg. 44, n.º 1250).

and the Herrán report (published in English, in London, to be disseminated in the United Kingdom in 1938).

Radio Salamanca broadcasted a message under the title "Agirre Lies" reproduced in several Francoist newspapers such as *Proa* in León, on April 29, 1937: "It is not the first time that Aguirre, 'boss' of the Republic of Euzkadi,[2] lies. Aguirre has declared today that the foreign aviation supporting the nationalist forces in Spain has bombed Gernika that as a result of it has been set afire, in order to inflict the biggest morale impact in the Basques. Aguirre lies. He lies and he knows it very well. First, there is not any German or foreign air force in the Nationalist Spain.[3] There is Spanish aviation, noble and heroic Spanish aviation, which has to fight continuously with the red aircraft, which are Russian and French and are piloted by foreign aviators. Secondly, Gernika has not been set afire by us. Franco's Spain does not set fires. The incendiary torch is a monopoly of those peoples that burnt Irun and have burnt Eibar and those who tried to burn the defenders of the Alcázar of Toledo alive. If we did not know that Aguirre knows that he is lying, as what he is, an ordinary delinquent, we would remind him that among those who fight on the front in Bizkaia, next to the

---

2.   Euzkadi or Euskadi in modern Basque characters is the Basque Country.

3.   The areas of Spain controlled by the National Movement.

'Gudaris,'[4] there are Asturian miners, professionals of destruction by the flame and the gasoline, and the barbaric dynamite of the Marxist violence, with whose collaboration Aguirre has wanted to remain as a king. We have respected Guernica not only for being Guernica, Basques of good faith, we have respected Guernica as we respect everything being Spanish and everything that must be, in a very short time, the only and true Spain."[5]

As reporter Noel Monks said: "Franco told the world there were none of his planes up that day, because of bad weather. I'm telling the world now that there were. I saw them. My two colleagues saw them. Six thousand inhabitants of Guernica saw them. And Monday, April 26th, was the sunniest day of all I spent on the Basque front. I'm not calling Franco a liar. Maybe he didn't know the Germans were up. Franco's German allies of the air work independently of Salamanca. I think their strafe of Guernica was done entirely off their own bat. I was among the ruins of Guernica one hour after the raiders had done their work. I wandered all over them, as far as I was able: the whole town was in flames. I saw bodies in the fields spotted with machine-gun bullets. I interviewed twenty or thirty survivors. They all told the same tale. Those who could speak. Some of them

---

4. Basque soldiers.

5. Proa, 126, León, April 29, 1937.

could only point skywards, put their hands over their ears and rock to and fro in terror. I went back to Bilbao and wrote my story. I was back at Guernica at day-break. I saw 600 bodies. Nurses, children, farmers, old women, girls, old men, babies. All dead, torn, and mutilated. Basque soldiers were getting the bodies from the wreckage, many of them weeping. I came to what had been an air-raid shelter. In it were the remains of fifty women and children. A bomb had dropped right through the house into the cellar. Does Franco expect the world to believe that fifty women and children fled into an air-raid shelter when their house was mined? Or trapped themselves below there while the house above them was set alight?"[6]

---

6.   Noel Monks, "I Saw the German Planes Bomb Guernica," *Daily Express*, London, May 1, 1937, 10.

25

Negationism and Reductionism

But in spite of the fact that reporters of the reputation of George Steer or Noel Monks who "saw 600 bodies," it has been repeated that the deaths in Gernika do not exceed 126, 250 or 300.

The official truth of the Franco dictatorship during thirty-nine years was that Gernika has not been bombed but burned by the "reds" in retreat. The mere mention that Gernika had been bombed could be punished with heavy fines or even imprisonment. As one witness of the bombing recounted: "After the bombing, the new priest repeated to the parishioners from the pulpit, in Castilian, that they should purge their sin with severe penances, for having sprayed Gernika with gasoline they had reduced their homes to ashes and to rubble the whole of the town. One day, having listened to the sermon in silence, two women went to the sacristy and tried to explain to the priest, privately, that they had not burned Gernika, that it had been Franco's planes that had destroyed their homes. The priest asked them to leave the church, with harsh words. In the morning, the Civil Guard went to their homes, forced them to go outside and shaved their hair off, in front of their houses, out in the street. Later, they walked them with their hands tied behind their backs all over Gernika and sentenced them in a summary trial to 36 months of imprisonment, of which they served 27."[1]

Gernika destroyed.

This campaign of official denial (negationism), one of the most long lasting official lies among those recorded in the twentieth-century Europe, has led from the end of the dictatorship

---

1.   Irujo, *El Gernika de Richthofen*, 478.

in 1975 to a reductionist school, tending to accept that a bombing occurred but minimizing its effects: reduction of Spanish and Italian participation through the assumption that it was an operation organized and executed solely by the German command without Franco's knowledge and that, consequently, the order to bomb Gernika did not come from Franco; reduction of the number of aircraft involved and the number of bombs dropped; reduction of the level of material destruction, and reduction of the number of deaths that Ricardo de la Cierva estimated at "a dozen" and Jesús Salas at 126.

Father Eusebio Arronategi, eyewitness of the bombing, telling what he saw in the radio in May 1937.

Reductionists also have claimed that the bombing was not a terror bombing but a strategic bombing. Wolfram von Richthofen was the first to note in his war diary that Gernika was a strategic target, since retreating troops from Markina or Eibar had to pass through the town. The objective of the bombing would therefore have been to obstruct with tons of rubble the retreat of the Basque battalions through Gernika. With no other means of escape, the Basque infantry units would have been bagged in the triangle formed by Markina, Eibar, and Gernika, at the mercy of the attackers.[2] All of which unsurprisingly never occurred.

2.   Maier, *Guernica*, 128.

26

Franco, Father and Adopted Son of Gernika

The regime used reconstruction as a means of propaganda. As reproduced by the regime's *Reconstrucción* magazine: "Let's put an end to so much evil [the affirmation that Gernika had been bombed] with the maximum good that is kindness, truth and justice."[1] Franco appeared through the propaganda channels of the dictatorship as "the architect of peace."

In August 1939, the Government of Bizkaia commissioned the sculptor José M. Garrós to make three wooden crucifixes from the tree of Gernika to be handed to the Pope, to Franco, and to have at the assembly hall of the Government

---

1. Dirección General de Regiones Devastadas y Reparaciones. Comisión de Vizcaya, *Ayuntamiento adoptado de Guernica. Relación de edificios de carácter público destruidos por acción de guerra, formulada en cumplimiento de la orden de 7 de octubre de 1939, año de la victoria*, Bilbao, November 10, 1939, 31-32.

itself. Coinciding with the reception of the cross, Franco granted by virtue of the decree of October 21, 1939 to Gernika the benefits of an "adopted town." The reconstruction works would be in charge of the General Directorate of Devastated Regions of the Ministry of Government headed by Ramón Serrano Suñer.

As recorded in the report of Gonzalo Cárdenas, architect of General Directorate of Devastated Regions, Gernika had in April 1937 a total of 318 buildings of which 271 were totally destroyed while the rest were affected by different considerations. The 271 houses destroyed by the bombing of Gernika constitute 85.22 percent of the buildings in Gernika and 67.58 percent of the total buildings entirely destroyed in the whole of Bizkaia (excluding Bilbao). Cárdenas estimated that the value of the buildings destroyed in its entirety rose to 11,940,791 pesetas. This supposes a 34.1 percent of the total expenses produced by the damages suffered in the whole of Bizkaia (that was calculated in 35 million pesetas), without counting Bilbao.[2]

By virtue of the decree of September 23, 1939, the Franco "adopted" towns and cities that had suffered serious damage during the war "to facilitate and organize the national reconstruction."[3] The regime authorities

2.   Ministerio de Gobernación. Dirección General de Regiones Devastadas. Comisión de Vizcaya, *Reconstrucción de la villa de Guernica. Memoria*, 1940, 2-3 and 11.

3.   Boletín Oficial del Estado, No. 274, October 1, 1939,

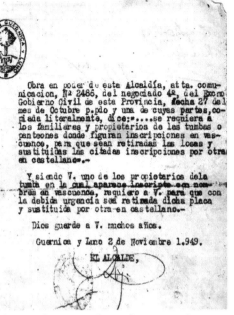

*Order of the Spanish authorities of 1949
to the people in Gernika to remove all
inscriptions in Basque from the tombsto
es at the cemetery and to replace them for
others written in Spanish.*

appointed by Franco would enjoy full powers of
expropriation over land, lots, and property and
rights of all kinds. A period of no more than fifteen days was granted to families who had lost
their homes during a bombing to claim legal
ownership of their properties. Thus, the people
considered "non-adept" to the regime did not
have the opportunity to claim their properties.

5489-5490.

With the expropriation materialized, the state built low-cost, low-quality housing that would later be rented or sold to their former or new owners. The first phases of the works were carried out using battalions of POWs and subsequently the adjudication of the works was made by designation. Finally, the redundant benefit of the sale of the houses took place in the context of a corrupt administration.

Coinciding with the end of one of the phases of the reconstruction process, on February 13, 1946, the city council of Gernika decided to name Franco "adoptive son" of the town, to engrave on a silver plaque this designation and to offer a gold medal to Franco, "Caudillo de la Reconstrucción" ("Reconstruction's leader") or on October 23, 1946, Franco received the municipal corporation of Gernika in El Pardo Palace, which informed him of the agreement of the city council and granted him the medal of the reconstruction. The one who had proclaimed himself as the adoptive father of Gernika had now also become his adopted son.

In 1949 the mayor of the town, Vicente Rojo, forced the owners of cemeteries with inscriptions in the Basque language in the Gernika cemetery to remove them and to replace them with others written in Spanish. Coinciding with the six hundredth anniversary of Gernika and in commemoration of the "thirty years of peace" of the regime, on February 2, 1966, the city council of Gernika granted the town's gold and diamond medal to Franco. On March 23, Franco received the delegation in El Pardo where the dictator received the medal and was informed of his appointment as President of the Board of Honor for the celebration of the Sixth Centenary of the Foundation of Gernika.

In short, Gernika was destroyed, expropriated, and sold at public auction for profit while Franco was presented through the propaganda channels of the regime as a benefactor, leader of the reconstruction, architect of peace, adoptive father, and adopted son of those towns that had suffered the incendiary torch of "reds and separatists."

27

Gernika:
City of Peace

The city of Gernika would need to endure many long years of systematic violence, dictatorship, and cultural repression following the devastating story told here. It was only in 1997 that the German government apologized for its role in the bombing, in a letter sent by German Chancellor Herzog to the survivors of the bombing. The survivors, having lived through the worst of human-made hells, responded:

> And they rained down fire, shrapnel and death on us. And they destroyed our town. And that night we couldn't go back home for our supper, or sleep in our beds. We had no home anymore. We had no house. But that event, which was so incomprehensible to us, left no feelings of hate or vengeance

in us—only a huge, immense desire for peace, and for such events never to happen again. A flag of peace should rise up from the ruins of what was our town for all the peoples of the world.[1]

---

1.   From the website of the Gernika Peace Museum, www.museodelapaz.org/docu_bombardeo.php,   accessed May 10, 2018.

Bibliography

Brett-Smith, Richard. *Hitler's Generals.* San Rafael, CA: Presidio Press, 1976.

Cloud, Yvonne, and Ellis, Richard. *The Basque Children in England. An Account of Their Life at North Stoneham Camp.* London: Victor Gollancz Ltd., 1937.

Cockburn, Claud. *I, Claud . . . : The Autobiography of Claud Cockburn.* New York: Penguin, 1967.

Corum, James S. *Wolfram von Richthofen: Master of the German Air War.* Lawrence: University Press of Kansas, 2008.

De la Cierva, Ricardo. "Guernica: los documentos contra el mito." In *Nueva y definitiva historia de la guerra civil.* Madrid: DINPE, 1986.

Elosegi, Joseba. *Quiero morir por algo.* Barcelona: Plaza y Janés, 1977.

Galland, Adolf. *Die Ersten und die Letzten: die Jagdflieger im zweiten Weltkrieg.* Darmstadt: F. Schneekluth, 1953.

———. *The First and the Last: The German Fighter Force in World War II.* London: Methuen, 1955.

Die Ersten und die Letzten: die Jagdflieger im zweiten Weltkrieg. Darmstadt: F. Schneekluth, 1953.

Gallego, José Andrés, and Pazos, Antonio M., eds. *Documentos de la guerra civil. 5: Abril–Mayo de 1937.* Madrid: CESIC, 2003.

Gamboa, José María, and Jean-Claude Larronde, eds. *La guerra civil en Euzkadi: 136 testimonios inéditos recogidos por José Miguel de Barandiarán.* Bidasoa: Milafranga, 2005.

Iribarren, José María. *Con el general Mola: Escenas y aspectos inéditos de la Guerra Civil.* Zaragoza: Librería General, 1937.

Irujo, Xabier. "Bonbaketa kanpaina Enkarterrin." In *"Itxaropena iñoiz ez da galtzen": Encartaciones. 1937: Los últimos meses de la guerra civil en Euskadi.* Edited by Javier Barrio, et al. Bilbao: Bizkaiko Batzar Nagusiak, 2017.

———. "Bombardeos en Euskadi (1936-1937)." In*Senderos de la memoria: Relación de espacios vinculados a la memoria de la guerra civil y el exilio.* 2 volumes. Edited by Joseba Agirreazkuenaga and Mikel Urkijo. Leioa: Grupo de investigación Biography & Parliament de la Universidad del País Vasco, 2016.

———. *El Gernika de Richthofen: Un ensayo de bombardeo de terror*. Gernika: Gernikako Bakearen Museoa Fundazioa/Gernika-Lumoko Udala, 2012.

———. *Genocidio en Euskal Herria*. Iruñea-Pamplona: Nabarralde, 2015.

———. *Gernika 1937: The Market Day Massacre*. Reno: University of Nevada Press, 2014.

———. *Gernika: 26 de abril de 1937*. Barcelona: Crítica, 2018.

Isla, José Francisco. *Compendio de la historia de España*. Madrid: Compañía General de Impresores y Libreros, 1845.

Iturralde, Juan [pseud. Juan Jose Usabiaga Irazustabarrena]. *El catolicismo y la cruzada de Franco*. Vienne: EGI Indarra, 1960,

Iturria, Joxe. *Memorias de Guerra*. Gernika: Gernika-Lumoko udala, 2013.

Jiménez de Aberasturi, Luis M., and Jiménez de Aberasturi, Juan C. *La guerra en Euskadi*. Donostia-San Sebastián: Txertoa, 2007.

Kay, Antony L., and Couper, Paul. *Junkers Aircraft and Engines, 1913-1945*. London: Putnam Aeronautical Books, 2004.

Maier, Klaus A. *Guernica. La intervención alemana en España y el "caso Guernica."* Madrid: Sedmay, 1976.

Medlicott, W. N., and Dakin Douglas, eds. *Documents on British Foreign Policy (1919-1939), Second Series, Volume XVIII, European Affairs (January 2-June 30, 1937)* London: Her Majesty's Stationery Office, 1980.

Mitcham, Samuel W. *Hitler's Commanders: Officers of the Wehrmacht, the Luftwaffe, the Kriegsmarine, and the Waffen-SS*. Lanham, MD: Rowman & Littlefield, 2012.

Múgica, Mateo. *Imperativos de mi conciencia: Carta abierta al presbítero D. José Miguel de Barandiarán*. Buenos Aires : Liga de Amigos de los Vascos, [1945?]

Neitzel, Sönke, and Welzer, Harald, eds. *Soldaten: On Fighting, Killing, and Dying. The Secret World War II Transcripts of German POWs*. Brunswick: Scribe Publications, 2012.

Nowarra, Heinz J. *Junkers Ju 52, Aircraft & Legend*. Newbury Park, CA: Haynes, 1987.

Olabarria, Zigor. *Gerra Zibila Otxandion*. Donostia-San Sebastián: Eusko Ikaskuntza, 2011.

Preston, Paul. *La muerte de Guernica*. Barcelona: Debate, 2017.

———. *The Spanish Holocaust: Inquisition and Extermination in Twentieth-Century Spain*. London: HarperCollins Publishers Ltd., 2008.

———. *The Destruction of Guernica*. London: HarperCollins Publishers Ltd., 2017. E-book edition.

Preston, Paul, and Mackenzie, Ann L., eds. *The Republic Besieged: Civil War in Spain 1936-1939*. Edinburgh: Edinburgh University Press, 1996.

Reig Tapia, Alberto, *Ideología e historia: sobre la represión franquista y la guerra civil*. Madrid: Akal, 1986.

Salas, Jesús. *Guernica*. Madrid: Rialp, 1987.

Smallwood, William. *The Day Guernica Was Bombed* (Gernika: Gernika-Lumoko udala, 2012.

Southworth, Herbert R. *Guernica! Guernica!: A Study of Journalism, Diplomacy, Propaganda, and history*. Berkeley: University of California Press, 1977.

Steer, George L. *The Tree of Gernika: A Field Study of Modern War*. London: Hodder and Stoughton Ltd., 1938.

Talón, Vicente. *El holocausto de Guernica*. Barcelona: Plaza & Janés, 1987.

Viñas, Ángel. "Epílogo [a la nueva edición de la obra de Herbert Southworth, *La destrucción de Guernica*]." Granada: Comares, 2013.

Weltman, John J. *World Politics and the Evolution of War*. Baltimore: Johns Hopkins University Press Press, 1995.